Borderlands in East and Southeast Asia

This book provides a glimpse into the different emergent borderland prototypes in East and Southeast Asia, with illustrative cases and discussions. Asia has contained a number of reactivated border zones since the end of the Cold War; borders which have witnessed ever greater human activity, concerning trade, commerce, tourism, and other forms of money-related activities such as shopping, gambling, and job-seeking. Through seven borderland cases, the contributors to this volume analyse how the changing political economy and the regional and international politics of Asia have shaped and reshaped borderland relations and produced a few essential prototypes of borderland in Asia, such as reopened borders and re-activated economic zones; reintegrated but "separated" border cities; porous borderlands; and abstruse borderlands. This book aims to bring about further discussions of borderland development and governance, and how these actually inform and shape state-state and state-city relations across borders and regional politics.

This book was originally published as a special issue of *Asian Anthropology*.

Yuk Wah Chan is associate professor in the Department of Asian and International Studies at City University of Hong Kong. She works with a wide range of scholars and her research interests cover borderland, migration, tourism, food, heritage, death, and identity.

Brantly Womack is C.K. Yen Professor of Foreign Affairs at the University of Virginia, USA. He is the author of *Asymmetry and International Relationships* (2016), *China among Unequals* (2010), and *China and Vietnam: The Politics of Asymmetry* (2006).

Borderlands in East and Southeast Asia

Emergent Conditions, Relations and Prototypes

Edited by
Yuk Wah Chan and Brantly Womack

LONDON AND NEW YORK

First published 2018
by Routledge
2 Park Square, Milton Park, Abingdon, Oxon, OX14 4RN, UK

and by Routledge
711 Third Avenue, New York, NY 10017, USA

Routledge is an imprint of the Taylor & Francis Group, an informa business

© 2018 The Department of Anthropology, The Chinese University of Hong Kong

All rights reserved. No part of this book may be reprinted or reproduced or utilised in any form or by any electronic, mechanical, or other means, now known or hereafter invented, including photocopying and recording, or in any information storage or retrieval system, without permission in writing from the publishers.

Trademark notice: Product or corporate names may be trademarks or registered trademarks, and are used only for identification and explanation without intent to infringe.

British Library Cataloguing in Publication Data
A catalogue record for this book is available from the British Library

ISBN 13: 978-1-138-09634-9

Typeset in Times New Roman
by RefineCatch Limited, Bungay, Suffolk

Publisher's Note
The publisher accepts responsibility for any inconsistencies that may have arisen during the conversion of this book from journal articles to book chapters, namely the possible inclusion of journal terminology.

Disclaimer
Every effort has been made to contact copyright holders for their permission to reprint material in this book. The publishers would be grateful to hear from any copyright holder who is not here acknowledged and will undertake to rectify any errors or omissions in future editions of this book.

Contents

Citation Information vii
Notes on Contributors ix

Introduction – Not merely a border: borderland governance, development and transborder relations in Asia
Yuk Wah Chan and Brantly Womack 1

1. Borders, boundaries, horizons and Quemoy in an asymmetric world
   Brantly Womack 10

2. Mobile North Korean women and their places in the Sino-North Korea borderland
   Sung Kyung Kim 22

3. The Thai-Burmese borderland: mobilities, regimes, actors and changing political contexts
   Petra Dannecker and Wolfram Schaffar 38

4. Mongla and the borderland politics of Myanmar
   Tharaphi Than 58

5. "Trust facilitates business, but may also ruin it": the hazardous facets of Sino-Vietnamese border trade
   Caroline Grillot 75

6. A tale of two borderlands: material lucidity and deep play in the transborder tourism space in Hong Kong and Macao
   Yuk Wah Chan 92

Index 113

Citation Information

The chapters in this book were originally published in *Asian Anthropology*, volume 15, issue 2 (August 2016). When citing this material, please use the original page numbering for each article, as follows:

Introduction
Not merely a border: borderland governance, development and transborder relations in Asia
Yuk Wah Chan and Brantly Womack
Asian Anthropology, volume 15, issue 2 (August 2016), pp. 95–103

Chapter 1
Borders, boundaries, horizons and Quemoy in an asymmetric world
Brantly Womack
Asian Anthropology, volume 15, issue 2 (August 2016), pp. 104–115

Chapter 2
Mobile North Korean women and their places in the Sino-North Korea borderland
Sung Kyung Kim
Asian Anthropology, volume 15, issue 2 (August 2016), pp. 116–131

Chapter 3
The Thai-Burmese borderland: mobilities, regimes, actors and changing political contexts
Petra Dannecker and Wolfram Schaffar
Asian Anthropology, volume 15, issue 2 (August 2016), pp. 132–151

Chapter 4
Mongla and the borderland politics of Myanmar
Tharaphi Than
Asian Anthropology, volume 15, issue 2 (August 2016), pp. 152–168

Chapter 5
"Trust facilitates business, but may also ruin it": the hazardous facets of Sino-Vietnamese border trade
Caroline Grillot
Asian Anthropology, volume 15, issue 2 (August 2016), pp. 169–185

CITATION INFORMATION

Chapter 6
A tale of two borderlands: material lucidity and deep play in the transborder tourism space in Hong Kong and Macao
Yuk Wah Chan
Asian Anthropology, volume 15, issue 2 (August 2016), pp. 186–206

For any permission-related enquiries please visit:
http://www.tandfonline.com/page/help/permissions

Notes on Contributors

Yuk Wah Chan is associate professor in the Department of Asian and International Studies, City University of Hong Kong. Her research interests cover international migration, borderland, tourism, identity, food, and death studies.

Petra Dannecker is professor of Development Studies and Sociology at the Department of Development Studies, University of Vienna, Austria. Her research focuses on globalization and migration processes, gender studies as well as methodologies and qualitative methods.

Caroline Grillot currently holds a research associate position in the School of Social Sciences at the University of Manchester, UK. Her research interests are social margins in China, including ethnic folklorisation, underground artistic communities, and cross-border Sino-Vietnamese marriages.

Sung Kyung Kim is assistant professor at the University of North Korean Studies in Seoul, South Korea.

Wolfram Schaffar is professor of Development Studies and Political Science at the Department of Development Studies, University of Vienna, Austria.

Tharaphi Than is assistant professor at Northern Illinois University, USA. Her research interests include women, censorship, and print media of Myanmar.

Brantly Womack is C.K. Yen Professor of Foreign Affairs in the Woodrow Wilson Department of Politics at the University of Virginia, USA. His research focuses on international relations.

Not merely a border: borderland governance, development and transborder relations in Asia

Yuk Wah Chan and Brantly Womack

The anthropology of borderlands

Borderlands are geographical places demarcated and defined by state-designed boundaries. Borderland communities, lying on the margin of more than one state, are thus existing in different development modes and terms of governance. Often, they are (physically) closer to a foreign regime and farther away from the central power of their own governments. People living in the borderlands are acquainted with different regimes of power, and may be skillful users of more than one language and currency for daily interaction and exchange.

Anthropologists have been actively studying borders and borderlands, not only because many borderlands have been neglected in research, but also because they are where anthropologists find concentrated marginalized groups (such as refugees) and minorities, intriguing cross-border state relations and human interactions and mixed and blurred identities. Borderland ethnographies also often provide interesting stories of alternative voices and views of state relations, history, culture, and identity that deviate from what has been defined by the state (Chang 2014; Chan 2013; Harris 2013; van Schendel 2005). The borderland is indeed a spatial variance of international relations (Chan 2013, 123).

While borders are themselves defining and delimiting state power and sovereignty, they are at the same time sites that constantly challenge and negotiate such power. Borders and boundaries are often imagined as hard and enclosing frontiers, yet many of them are, in reality, porous (Horstmann and Wadley 2006; Tagliacozzo 2005; Walker 1999; Wilson and Donnan 1999, 1998). Borderlanders can be active "border-crossers" who make use of such skills to challenge state control and discourses on "boundaries" in order to work on the improvement of life chances and livelihoods. In the unstable war-torn border zone in northern Myanmar, for example, borderlanders are quick to exploit short-term peace and transborder differences. Even in the worst cases of hostile and militarized borders, such as the island of Quemoy in the Taiwan Strait during the Cold War, daily reality is defined by being on the edge of the state and residents are suspect because of their transborder ties (Szonyi 2008). The anthropology of borderlands thus helps maintain and spread voices and perspectives less heard and known of, and produce knowledge and "interstices of culture" that "supplement, challenge and contrast views from the centre" (Chan 2013, 127; also see Thongchai Winichakul 1994).

This special issue intertwines the anthropology of borderlands with the political concepts of governance and development, and employs an actor-oriented approach to examine a few borderlands in Asia. Through this approach, we are able to attend to the variety of different political economic contexts for development and how people – the subject of development – are responding, reacting, circumventing, and resisting such a structural factor as the borderland that has acted on them. The borderland, in this sense, is a specific place/space for us to examine varied forms of governance and development, deviating, to a large extent, from the usual ways that governance and development have been discussed.

Borderland governance and asymmetries

We use the concept of "borderland governance" to weave together a number of Asian borderland cases that analyze very different sets and types of data. Although governance has been a catchword in the academic world, especially in public administration and development literature, not many have applied this to the study of borderlands. For those who have, they have mostly attended to state behavior. As Yu Keping argues (Yu 2015), "governance" can be distinguished from "government" in several ways. Government authority is unitary, while governance involves different levels and venues of authority. And although governance implies instrumentality toward given goals, it requires interaction with civil society and local populations for its effectiveness. "Government" is concerned with formal structure and process; "governance" is concerned with interaction and outcomes.

While governance is never transparent, borderland governance is more than national government at its periphery (Brunet-Jailly 2013; Donnan and Haller 2000). A borderland is a place of contact. Its realities on the ground are not simply outcomes of national policies on each side, but instead creatively interact with opportunities and constraints. Borderland communities are often skillful at appropriating and posing canny challenges to state authorities and policies. Whether viewed from the perspective of a single border trader or an entire bi-national region, they are lively, fluid places. They are contingent on their national definitions, but identities of – and within – borderlands shape themselves as they navigate between the opportunities opened by contact and the constraints of their situation (Donnan and Wilson 1994; Wilson and Donnan 1999). Asymmetry is a root feature of borderland governance because of the relationship of periphery to center, as well as that of states. Moreover, (inter)national asymmetries of power, capabilities and resources shape the structure of border contact and governance (Taylor 2008; Womack 2006, 2004). Both the state and individuals are sensitive about and acquainted with such asymmetries and their changes. As stated by Chan (2013, 6), border regions often form "a frontier 'thermometer' that detects changing inter-state relations."

For us, borderland governance serves as a framework broad enough to cover both state and non-state actors. The special issue deals with a wide spectrum of issues, ranging from economic development through different forms of cross-border exchange (such as trade, investment, and marriage) to trans-border human flows (from borderland tourism, to migration, to human trafficking). Border governance inevitably touches on borderland legislation and policies that regulate cross-border activities as well as state relations that shape such policies and activities. We stress that borderland governance has often involved the acts of different categories of borderlanders. The cases included in the issue handle myriad interactive dynamics between state and non-state, local and global actors, and their intertwined relationships at the border. The articles in this special issue also examine a myriad of border relations and social space constantly created and recreated at the margins and across borders. Borderland studies provide alternative perspectives to the study of the state – understanding the center from the margin – geographically and ideologically (Taylor 2007; Thongchai Winichakul 1994); this special issue's exploration into borderland governance likewise offers new lenses for understanding governance that involve multiple border-crossing relations and actors.

An actor-oriented approach

Borderland governance immediately involves inter-state relations, transborder interactions, compatibility and incompatibility (of social, political, and economic systems), value and ideological differences, power asymmetry, identity shifts, and constant mobility. Despite the many benefits of the traditional institutional approach for examining state relations, we propose an actor-oriented approach that speaks to and about those who act within such state relations and their interactive dynamics. Hence, we do not just look at state level acts – policies, border regulations, and discourses. We employ a dynamic approach to look into how different sectors of actors at the border act and interact with each other (Wilson and Donnan 1999, 1998). While two neighboring countries may work out complementary trade policies regulating cross-border commodity exchange and taxation, borderlanders' reaction to such policies bring unexpected effects to the original intention of regulation. Indeed, structure and agency often intertwine, affecting each other in varied ways (Brunet-Jailly 2013; Horstmann and Wadley 2006); and borderlanders are those who live their everyday life at the borderland.

Different borderlands exhibit different levels of control and openness (Alvarez 1995; Chavez 1994; Cunningham and Heyman 2004; Ganster et al. 1997; Gilles et al. 2013; Lorey 1999; Martinez 1994; Ross 1978; Smith 1998; Staudt and Spencer 1998). In this issue, we pay attention to the different kinds of borders: restrictive, and relatively more open, as well as borders-in-transition. We discuss the kinds of control and regulation at border regions which neighboring governments put into practice. Whether at restrictive or open borders, we find that borderlanders often actively respond to such restrictions as well as to newly earned liberties of border-crossing. Informal border-crossing is more commonly found than could be imagined from official accounts. Thus, although borders represent the state's sovereignty and power – an important part of state identity – it is here that violation of state control often appears, and local, contingent identities emerge. Borderlanders are those who are familiar with all the "flexibilities" at inflexible borders. Whether at restrictive or relatively open borders, borderlanders actively respond to such limitation and openness in their idiosyncratic ways (Walker 1999, 17; Donnan and Wilson 1994: 11–12).

Transborder relations and development

Borders necessarily breed differences and asymmetries. Besides the asymmetries that states and state relations entail and bear, border differences also assume an asymmetry and dynamics of identity (Brambilla 2007; Chan 2013; Staudt and Spencer 1998; Wilson and Donnan 1998). Wilson and Donnan argue that borderlands are where state-defined power, history and identity are "continuously negotiated and reinterpreted through the dialectics of everyday life among all people who live at them" (1994, 11). One may assume that at border areas, frequent interaction across borders will bring familiarity of interchangeable identities and mixed ways of living. Yet border areas also witness the worst types of stereotypes and conflicts due to intensified border interactions (Chan 2013; Grillot 2012). The contingency of border realities can lead to rigidities of identity as well as to hybridization, which "define" people and are "used" by the people as well. Border relations are concerned with the shifting discourses of border identities at different levels (individuals, families, specific groups, and the state), and how they affect daily border-crossing, interaction, and livelihood.

Development is a very broad concept and involves all kinds of economic and political policies that would help stabilize a place's environment and enhance economic growth. However, most often, while policies and rules may provide a general environment to a certain place, and define the status (such as citizenship) of individuals, the actual work of livelihood has often been shaped by different decisions and strategies of individuals and groups that respond to such policies and rules and thus create new political and economic relations between individuals and families, and between individuals and the state and across borders (Chou 2006; Staudt 1998). Borders are margins and boundaries, which can be interpreted as spaces of both dangers and opportunities. It is also at borderlands that governance, inter-state relations, and development become most agile and fragile.

Translocal border space

Border-crossing mobility necessarily incurs a pantheon of space that evokes negotiation and contestation of interests, ideologies, status, and identity. Borders generate new social spaces (which can be real or imagined); borders also split social spaces. A border can be defined as a state's intervention into overlapping social domains, such as family, business, religion, and livelihood, for the sake of establishing and validating sovereignty. State regulation of border thus involves much discussion of legality and illegality. Yet, the implementation of border control at the same time brings ambiguity about such "legalization" – the institutionalized framework for border-crossing. Borderland families which actively conduct border-crossings and make transborder familial connections and personalized trading relationships, continuously create translocal social spaces, for which "legalization" may or may not cater (Collins 2013; Smith 1998; Smith and Guarnizo 1998). While they are constantly subject to bilateral national control, they are also often making "un-institutionalized" border-crossings – usually understood as informal border-crossing at "informal" border exits. Informality at borderlands is insufficiently appreciated because it must be experienced on-site. It can be misleading to put this immediately into the domain of illegality. Border-crossing (including informal exit and entry, massive refugee exodus, and individual sneaking) is a space where the state is negotiated, contested, and shaped.

Asian borderlands

Reactivated border zones

Asian borderlands offer a peculiar landscape for the understanding of governance and development. This is not only because many of these borderlands have been sites for political struggles and military conflicts; they are also spaces that have witnessed many shifts and shuffles of powers and regimes of regulation (Chapmen et al. 1992; Evans et al. 2000; Gu and Womack 2000; Horstmann 2011; Roper 2000; van Schendel and

Maaker 2014; van Schendel 2005; Walker 1999; Womack 2000, 1994). While some of these borderlands still carry the legacies of colonialism, others were once closed or semi-closed and reopened in recent years (Chan 2013). They are also now and then "under stress" due to contingent political struggles and diplomatic standstill. At times when political divides have been mended, borderlands act as growth regions.

Asia, among other regions, accommodates extremely diverse political and economic systems. Borderlanders in Asia are mostly quick to exploit or capitalize on the newly developed borderland political economies and thereby work on improving their life chances and livelihoods. In short, to tie this temporal dimension back to the concept of asymmetries (of powers and identities), one will be open to the prism of asymmetric relationships at borderlands through multiple overlapping time-space domains and metaphors. All cases in this special issue offer views and sites of reality from the "margins," which are not merely alternatives from the border, but are taken as "central" and essential to provide a grounded understanding of governance, border-crossing, and development, as well as transborder relations.

Borderland prototypes

In this special issue, we bring together six different cases which show the dynamics and diversity of Asian borderlands. Rooted in the diverse political systems and cross-border relations in the region, these Asian borderlands offer a fascinating scene in terms of rapid shifts in state-state relationships, transborder interactions, and borderland development.

The cases included in this special issue manifest a few prototypes of Asian borderlands:

(1) Reopened borders and re-activated economic zones (this includes those between China and Vietnam as well as mainland China and Taiwan, both of which earlier suffered from a period of diplomatic standoff and immense political tension);
(2) Reintegrated but "separated" border cities (for example, Hong Kong and Macau, which were returned to China in the late 1990s, but were maintained as specially administered border cities of China);
(3) Porous borderlands (this includes the territories at the Thai-Burmese and Sino-Burmese borders, which have witnessed frequent informal, if not illegal, migrations);
(4) Abstruse borderlands (this is the case at the Sino-North Korean border region: although this border is usually perceived to be highly guarded and impenetrable, there have been border-crossing activities, especially conducted by North Korean women who took to the border to seek alternative survival paths).

Organization of papers

Brantly Womack, in this issue's first article, depicts a fascinating case of a military base-turned-tourist site. With the waning of the "fight back" ideology and discourse in Taiwan, and reduced antagonism between the PRC (People's Republic of China) and the ROC (Republic of China), Jinmen (Quemoy) – an island lying between mainland China and Taiwan – developed first into an exotic tourist destination for mainland Chinese tourists to expand their imaginations about a "political China" and then subsided into being a convenient excursion as cross-strait relations improved. Jinmen, a Taiwan-controlled borderland a few kilometers from mainland China, shows the full spectrum of borderland politics, from hostility to normalcy. Womack proposes a general conceptualization of borderlands and argues that there are three dimensions to any borderland: the locality of contact, the regulatory attempt to control and define activities, and the analytic framing of a certain area as a border area. Highlighting the asymmetric normal relationship between China and Taiwan crystallized in the touristic borderland of Quemoy, Womack attempts to unpack the political discourses and realities of civil war, peaceful unification, and development.

Sung Kyung Kim, in the next article, explores the border space at the China-North Korea borderland. Popular understanding of the life of North Koreans centers on their restricted movement controlled by the authoritarian North Korean state and their general suffering, with any border-crossing movements at the risk of their lives. Few have studied in detail the actual practices of border-crossing of the North Koreans who dwell at the borderlands. Contrary to general understandings of North Korean migrants, many North Koreans at the Sino-North Korea borderland cross the border (a border river) as a matter of everyday practice. They do not even bother to settle across the border, but instead enjoy mobility between the two sides of the borderland. This article thus contests the general restrictive stereotypes that frame North Korean mobility, and argues that these border-crossers are calculative agents actively balancing the costs and benefits of migration. A decision of migration often takes into account North Koreans' spatial perception, intimate human network of relatives, sense of familiarity with language, feelings and emotions for places and people, with little reference to political purges or economic deprivation usually depicted by the media.

Petra Dannecker and Wolfram Schaffar, in the next article, study the space of labor and refugee migration at the Thai-Burmese border region. Unlike most previous literature that focuses on the political and economic struggles of the refugees, their paper discusses how this borderland has turned into a playing field for local, national and international actors striving for different political and economic goals. A long-term haven for active refugees and dissidents, the Thai-Burmese borderlands have become important research sites for examining border politics and particular forms of development and governance under global influences.

Tharaphi Than, in her report, then captures a different kind of development in a border town along the China-Myanmar borderline. With increasing contacts across the border with the Chinese, Mongla, a border town in Myanmar, has been rapidly sinicized. Not only has the Chinese currency become the most common currency in the town, local resources, including land and forests, have been turned into Chinese properties. The town has also thrived through vices – gambling, prostitution, and drugs. Than probes into the new economy of this border town, and reveals the complex triangular relationships between the Chinese, Mongla leaders, and the central government of Myanmar.

Caroline Grillot, in her article, then examines the changing border relations arising from the thriving border trade and businesses between Vietnam and China. Looking deep into the strategies with which Chinese entrepreneurs deal with their Vietnamese business counterparts and Vietnam's sporadically revised trade policies, she explores trust discourses and practices among Vietnamese and Chinese trade partners and asks how exactly trade partners within different states can learn to trust each other at the borderlands. By looking into the work of money-exchangers at the "Wall Street" in Móng Cái, a Vietnamese border city on the Vietnam-China border, Grillot examines the daily interactive patterns of Chinese and Vietnamese and how both have been actively building "trust capital" for self-interest and for guarding against money traps. The paper has added an important ethnographic case to the literature of trust and business networks.

Yuk Wah Chan discusses the border cities of Hong Kong and Macau. While both have become part of China since the late 1990s, they are both largely self-administered, bearing the status of "special administrative regions" for 50 years. However, prior to becoming completely integrated with China, both cities have "merged" with China in terms of overflows of mainland Chinese visitors. Chan argues that this development of the two border cities has come about as a result of the problematic growth of the transitional political economy of China. Millions of Chinese tourists cross the border to collect daily consumer items from Hong Kong, while many of those crossing the China-Macau border do so to gamble. The article examines how Hong Kong has become a remedy for China's problematic "fake goods" market, and how Macau has come to the rescue of China's outflow of *renminibi* and acted as a space for the deep play of the risk-taking psyche of mainland Chinese.

References

Alvarez, Robert R. 1995. "The Mexican-US Border: The Making of an Anthropology of Borderlands." *Annual Review of Anthropology* 24: 447–470.

Brambilla, Chiara. 2007. "Borders and Identities/Border Identities: The Angola Namibia Border and the Plurivocality of the Kwanyama Identity." *Journal of Borderlands Studies* 22 (2): 21–38.

Brunet-Jailly, Emmanuel. 2013. "Power, Politics and Governance of Borderlands: The Structure and Agency of Power." In *Theorizing Borders through Analyses of Power Relationships*, edited by Peter Gilles, et al., 29–44. Bruxelles: P.I.E.-Peter Lang.

Chan, Yuk Wah. 2013. *Vietnamese-Chinese Relationships at the Borderlands: Trade, Tourism and Cultural Politics*. London: Routledge.

Chang, Wen-Chin. 2014. *Beyond Borders: Stories of Yunnanese Chinese Migrants of Burma*. Ithaca, NY: Cornell University Press.

Chapmen, E. C., Peter Hinton, and Jingrong Tan. 1992. "Cross-Border Trade between Yunnan and Burma, and the Emerging Mekong Corridor." *Thai-Yunnan Project Newsletter* 19: 15–19.

Chavez, Leo. 1994. "The Power of the Imagined Community: The Settlement of Undocumented Mexicans and Central Americans in the United States." *American Anthropologist* 96 (1): 52–73.

Chou, Cynthia. 2006. "Borders and Multiple Realities: The Orang Suku Laut of Riau, Indonesia." In *Centering the Margin: Agency and Narrative in Southeast Asian Borderlands*, edited by Alexander Horstmann, and R. Wadley, 111–134. New York: Berghahn Books.

Collins, Kimberly. 2013. "Life in the US–Mexican Border Region: Residents' Perceptions of the Place." *Journal of Borderlands Studies* 28 (1): 127–146.

Cunningham, H., and J. Heyman. 2004. "Introduction: Mobilities and Enclosures at Border." *Identities* 11 (3): 289–302.

Donnan, Hastings, and Dieter Haller. 2000. "Liminal No More: The Relevance of Borderland Studies." *Ethnologia Europaea* 30 (2): 7–22.

Donnan, Hastings, and Thomas Wilson, eds. 1994. *Border Approaches: Anthropological Perspectives on Frontiers*. Lanham: University Press of America.

Evans, Grant, Christopher Hutton, and Kuah Khun Eng, eds. 2000. *Where China Meets Southeast Asia: Social and Cultural Change in the Border Regions*. Singapore: Institute of Southeast Asian Studies.

Gilles, Peter, Harlan Koff, Carmen Maganda, and Christian Schulz, eds. 2013. *Theorizing Borders through Analyses of Power Relationships*. Bruxelles: P.I.E.-Peter Lang.

Ganster, Paul, et al., eds. 1997. *Borders and Border Regions in Europe and North America*. San Diego, CA: San Diego State University Press.

Grillot, Caroline. 2012. "Cross-Border Marriages between Vietnamese Women and Chinese Men: The Integration of Otherness and the Impact of Popular Representations." In *Wind over Water: Migration in an East Asian Context*, edited by D. Haines, K. Yamanaka, and S. Yamashita, 125–137. New York: Berghahn Books.

Gu, Xiaosong, and Brantly Womack. 2000. "Border Cooperation between China and Vietnam in the 1990s." *Asian Survey* 40 (6): 1042–1058.

Harris, Tina. 2013. *Geographical Diversions: Tibetan Trade, Global Transactions*. Athens: University of Georgia Press.

Horstmann, Alexander. 2011. "Borderlands and Border Studies in South-East Asia." *Austrian Journal of South-East Asian Studies* 4 (2): 203–214.

Horstmann, Alexander, and R. Wadley, eds. 2006. *Centering the Margin: Agency and Narrative in Southeast Asian Borderlands*. New York: Berghahn Books.

Lorey, David. 1999. *The US-Mexican Border in the Twentieth Century: A History of Economics and Social Transformation*. Wilmington: A Scholarly Resources.

Martinez, Oscar. 1994. *Border People: Life and Society in the US-Mexico Borderlands*. Tuscon: University of Arizona Press.

Roper, Christopher. 2000. "Sino-Vietnamese Relations and the Economy of Vietnam's Border Region." *Asian Survey* 40 (6): 1019–1041.

Ross, Stanley. 1978. *Views across the Border: The United States and Mexico*. Albuquerque: University of New Mexico Press.

Smith, Michael Petter and Luis Eduardo Guarnizo. 1998. "The Locations of Transnationalism." In *Transnationalism from below*, edited by Michael Petter Smith. and Luis Eduardo Guarnizo, 3–34. New Brunswick: Transaction Publishers.

Smith, Robert. 1998. "Transnational Localities: Communities, Technologies and the Politics of Membership within the Context of Mexico-US Migration." In *Encuentros Antropologicos: Power, Identity and Mobility in Mexican Society*, edited by Valentina Napolitano, and Xochite Leyva Solano, pp. 144–169. London: Institute of Latin American Studies, University of London.

Staudt, Kathleen. 1998. *Free Trade? Informal Economies at the US-Mexico Border*. Philadelphia, PA: Temple University Press.

Staudt, Kathleen, and David Spencer, eds. 1998. *The U.S.-Mexico Border: Transcending Divisions, Contesting Identities*. Boulder, CO: Lynnne Rienner.

Szonyi, Michael. 2008. *Cold War Island: Quemoy on the Front Line*. Cambridge: Cambridge University Press.

Tagliacozzo, Eric. 2005. *Secret Trades, Porous Borders: Smuggling and States along a Southeast Asian Frontier, 1865–1915*. New Haven, CT: Yale University Press.

Taylor, Fravel. 2008. *Strong Borders, Secure Nation: Cooperation and Conflict in China's Territorial Disputes*. Princeton, NJ: Princeton University Press.

Taylor, Philip. 2007. *Cham Muslims of the Mekong Delta: Place and Mobility in the Cosmopolitan Periphery*. Honolulu: University of Hawaii Press.

Thongchai Winichakul. 1994. *Siam Mapped: A History of the Geo-Body of a Nation*. Honolulu: University of Hawaii Press.

van Schendel, Willem. 2005. *The Bengal Borderland: Beyond State and Nation in South Asia*. London: Anthem Press.

van Schendel, Willem, and Erik de Maaker. 2014. "Asian Borderlands: Introducing Their Permeability, Strategic Uses and Meanings." *Journal of Borderlands Studies* 29 (1): 3–9.

Walker, Andrew. 1999. *The Legend of the Golden Boat: Regulation, Trade and Traders in the Borderlands of Laos, Thailand, China and Burma*. Surrey: Curzon Press.

Wilson, Thomas M., and Hastings Donnan. 1999. *Borders: Frontiers of Identity, Nation and State*. Oxford: Berg.
Wilson, Thomas M., and Hastings Donnan, eds. 1998. *Border Identities: Nation and State at International Frontiers*. Cambridge: Cambridge University Press.
Womack, Brantly. 2006. *China and Vietnam: The Politics of Asymmetry*. New York: Cambridge University Press.
Womack, Brantly. 2004. "Asymmetry Theory and China's Concept of Multipolarity." *Journal of Contemporary China* 13 (39): 351–366.
Womack, Brantly. 2000. "International Relationships at the Border of China and Vietnam: An Introduction." *Asian Survey* 40 (6): 981–986.
Womack, Brantly. 1994. "Sino-Vietnamese Border Trade: The Edge of Normalization." *Asian Survey* 34 (6): 495–512.
Yu, Keping. 2015. *Essays on the Modernization of State Governance*. Beijing: Social Science Academic Press.

Borders, boundaries, horizons and Quemoy in an asymmetric world[†]

Brantly Womack

> The diversity of borderland realities makes the necessity of general conceptualization particularly challenging. An interrelated conceptual triad is proposed and then applied to the experience of Quemoy Island (金门, Kinmen, Jinmen) from 1895 to the present. All borderlands are places in which contact is shaped by a standing and distinctive disparity, and the boundaries that both define and split the area create the rules of border gaming and the larger contingencies influencing border identities. Whether a village, a region, or a state is treated as a borderland – in other words, the horizons of focus – is determined by the analyst but on the basis of the realities of venue and governance. In Quemoy and most other border situations, asymmetries of power, resources, and capabilities provide an uneven ground for interactions and therefore shape the realities and perceptions of contact.

Border areas are among the most richly textured human spaces, bringing endless delights to adventurers and endless headaches to regulators. To pursue abstractions about them seems to be contrary to their nature. To ask the question, "what do all borderlands have in common?" appears to squeeze the life and uniqueness out of each one and to leave an uninteresting, leaden residue. It is nevertheless a necessary question. Terminological consistency requires attention to definitions, and, more importantly, a general conceptual model provides a framework for communicating, comparing, and articulating differences among cases and changes over time. The first task here is to try to formulate a conceptual scheme that would be true of all borderlands, anywhere. Not because they are all the same, but because if we call them all "borderlands" we must have some general feature in mind. While this philosophical anatomy of borderlands is pallid and lifeless, it will be applied to Quemoy, a borderland whose variety of experiences stretches the limits of conceptualization. We first lay out the bare bones of the conceptualization, for the sake of clarity, and then Quemoy adds the flesh. Finally we will consider the effects of asymmetry in structuring border interactions.

Border areas, boundaries, and horizons

With a little effort and imagination, every situation can be described as a border to something, or between two things. National borders are the most obvious, but there are frontiers of terrain, urbanization, ethnicity, political intensity, and so forth. Even

---

[†]An earlier version was presented as the keynote address at *Activated Borders: Reopenings, Ruptures, and Relationships*, 4th Conference of the Asian Borderlands Research Network, City University of Hong Kong, December 2014.

personalities can have borders. With such a flexibility of application, the question of what is or is not a border becomes meaningless. The better question is what is being claimed when we call something a borderland?

The challenge of defining a border is more complex than it might seem. It would be easy to take the position that, for instance, "a border is a place where two states meet," and to consider any other usages either incorrect or metaphorical. While that approach would distinguish the category of "border" from everything else, it would not tell us much about why borders are interesting, and why the usage of the term stretches beyond that "proper" categorization. It is rare that a researcher is simply contrasting a border to a non-border. Rather, it is the complexity of border reality that attracts attention. Definitional gate-keeping has its uses, but a more fruitful approach might be to reflect on why people are interested in what they call borders.

I argue that there are three elements or dimensions to the claim that something is a borderland. First, it is a venue of interactions based on differences. It involves a border area in which differences meet. Second, a border implies a distinction between a periphery and one or more centers. A border implies boundaries. Lastly, research about a particular border requires a framing, a horizon of discourse. I label these elements border areas, boundaries, and horizons. Their underlying general claim is that there is a significant and located difference in the borderland that merits attention.

The three elements of border areas, boundaries, and horizons constitute a conceptual model for borders and have utilities beyond mere categorization. To be sure, any sustained discussion of a border should involve or imply all three elements. Like a molecule, the elements can be distinguished, but all three are required for completeness. But the elements are not equally important in all cases and at all times. Rather, they are like the moments of a conceptual triad in Hegel's dialectic, related to one another and each fulfilling a distinct logical role.[1] As we will see in the case of Quemoy, it moved from a rather boundary-less situation of being the stepping-off point for emigration to the South China Sea to being a closed-off hyper-boundary during the Cold War. Research about Quemoy before 1947 fits well into the horizons of coastal China, while afterwards it became part of the Cold War, and more recently a border area between Taiwan and the Mainland. Exploration of the different salience of the elements moves the conceptualization of borders beyond mere categorization. We can move beyond the questions, "are the essential elements present?" "are we talking about a border?" to the more interesting questions, "how do the elements relate and change?" "what makes this border worth our attention and generally significant?"

Borders areas: venues of interactions presuming difference

A border area is a venue of interactions that presumes a significant gradient of difference. It is a place of a special kind of contact. For example, any market presumes a difference between buyer and seller, but these are roles that anyone can have and anyone can change. The peculiarity of a border market is that the different situations on either side of the border create a gradient that affects interactions. The gradient of difference, whatever that might consist of at a particular border, creates both the opportunities for contact and the urge felt by officials to govern interactions. Rice can be bought and sold in any market, but if the price of rice is higher in China than in Vietnam, in the border market rice will tend to be a popular item flowing only in one direction. Difference is not always a matter of price. Mainland Chinese come to Hong Kong to buy huge quantities of infant formula because of food safety scandals at home. Many resell the powder to Shenzhen wholesalers when they return across the border.

A border area does not have to lie between two centers. Any periphery with a located gradient of difference could be considered a border area. For example, coastal/ inland, agricultural/nomadic. One can consider the interactions between the centers and peripheries of William Skinner's macroregions of China as border interactions, though this might stretch the notion beyond its usual application (Skinner 1977). Basically, if one place has something that a neighboring place doesn't, then it is likely that there will be a gradient of interaction based on that difference at the place where they meet – the border area. In the case of a seaward border the "neighboring place" becomes non-specific, and in the case of emigration the gradient of difference pulls people out of the border venue.

A significant gradient of difference is not limited to commodities, and interactions are not limited to the exchange of goods. Border areas between ethnic groups or states are usually characterized by cultural interactions premised on difference. A border is a place where a fairly stable and distinct difference provides the framing tension of the fabric of interaction.

A periphery of central control can be viewed as a border area if there is a significant gradient of difference with the center. If two remote peripheries meet at a frontier then a border area can become an intermediate zone. Instead of a gradient of difference between the interactors themselves, the border frontier can be defined by a difference between the shared periphery and its various centers. An example would be a trans-border ethnic group engaged in smuggling. In contrast to the typical border area the internal interactions would be homogeneous but the interactions with centers would be based on difference. This would be a limit case for a border area because it would not be intersected by boundaries. But the difference between such an area and its surrounding centers would be the reason for treating it as a border area.

Boundaries: differentiation of identities and interests

The second element in the conceptual molecule of borders is the idea of boundary. Boundaries are the source and reality of the gradient of difference present in border areas. The second moment in a Hegelian triad is that of definition, of determining the limits of the first, and in most cases boundaries define the border. As James Scott has argued, there is an inevitable tension between mobility and governance (Scott 2009).

The liminality of borders creates an analogous urge for transparency and control on the part of the respective states, hence border checkpoints and visas. But it is not only the states that must define themselves. The borderland actors exist in a fluid and contingent environment that requires a constant recalibration of who they are and what they want. The term "boundaries" is felicitous because it suggests the challenge posed to identities by interactions based on difference. The interesting thing about the role of definition of identities and interests in border areas is that it is not the border area itself that is delimited; rather each interactor, facing the gradient of difference, must stake out his, her, or its identity and interests. Boundaries are posited by the different identities and interests of each side, and they meet in the middle of the border area – they bisect it. The border area is the place where bounded identities meet.

The most obvious boundaries are those marking political control. To some extent these boundaries create the differences that literally define border areas. The train stops here. Passports must be shown. And in most cases boundaries create the barriers that, by attempting to control contact, create and shape an interactive venue. As the concerns of border governance approach zero, as in the EU's Schengen system before the 2015 refugee crisis, the border area becomes less meaningful. There is less reason to cross, and fewer people stop or are stopped. By contrast, a frontier border area with diminished central control from any direction can develop its own identity distinct from its transnational situation. The difference between a border area and an interstitial state can sometimes be a matter of interpretation.

If a border is hostile or sealed and cross-border interaction is prohibited, then a border area is literally marginalized. It becomes the edge where one political identity confronts another, alien identity, militarized and impoverished by its loss of opportunities. While a locality in a rear area has a full circle of possible interaction, a sealed border has at best a half circle as well as the security distortions of being at the front line of confrontation. As the boundary becomes an absolute barrier, the border becomes an edge of authority rather than a border area.

In a "normal" border area, one where interaction occurs and is governed by both sides, the difference in governance shapes each side of the venue. If it is very tedious for anyone, including locals, to cross the border, then it will tend to be a rather sterile point of inspection and transshipment. If there is a difference in governance but border formalities are bearable then the border area itself will induce a clientele attracted by the different grass on the other side of the fence. If there is a special permissiveness for local, small-scale interaction, as on China's mainland borders (Chan 2013), it is likely that a third and more richly textured layer of localized interaction will be part of border life, involved with more formal international exchange but distinctive.

Just as commodities are not the only modality of border interaction, so politics is not the only modality of boundary governance. As groups take advantage of interactions outside their group, they must protect their particular interests and identities. Indeed, the presence of other groups requires additional definition of their own identity, beyond intergenerational socialization and subgroup rivalry. And perceived pressure from other groups requires governance of group boundaries. Contact requires groups to develop their own "foreign policy" and to manage the borders of their own identities. As with political boundary management, societal and cultural governance can run the gamut from self-isolation to uninhibited contact, though there are more options to specify different categories or targets of looser and tighter group concern.

Horizons: framing border areas

The third element in the conceptual molecule of borders, horizons, also fits well into the Hegelian triad of moments. The first element, the border venue, expresses the "thereness" of the border area, the location of interactions premised on difference. The second, boundaries, provides the counterposed definitions that delineate the different identities that meet as well as their patterns of interactions. In the third moment of framing, the observer posits that there is a *significant* locus of interaction based on a gradient of difference. The framing decision is an aesthetic judgment of the perceived coherence of border area reality. Different horizons are possible because the observer can focus on different dimensions of significance. To illustrate, a border area could be a local market on the China-Mongolian border, or adjoining border counties, or even Mongolia itself as a nexus between Russia and China. Framing is subjective in the sense that it is done by the observer, but significance is asserted on the basis of a venue of configured interaction. It is important to note that while it is up to the analyst to pick the framing, it is not simply a matter of analytic categorization. The claimed horizons must demarcate real contexts of interaction.

Quemoy (Kinmen, Jinmen, Chinmen, 金門, 金门)

The discussion thus far has been an attempt to construct a conceptual framework sufficiently abstract to be used to discuss any border. It aspires to be more than a "yes it is one/no it isn't one" categorization of border areas. Thus it is important to illustrate its utility by applying it to a case. However, since the point of the framework is to add an analytical dimension to the texture of border studies rather than to displace the thick description of its reality, I will first sketch the general situation of Quemoy and only afterwards directly address the elements of the framework.

Quemoy (see Figure 1) is a small island with an extraordinarily complex experience of border interactions. It has an area of 150 square kilometers (60 square miles) and a population of 120,000. Although it is part of Fujian Province and separated by only a few kilometers of water from Xiamen City, 160 kilometers across the Strait from Taiwan, it is also part of the Republic of China (ROC). The retreating Guomindang (KMT) army successfully defended it against the People's Liberation Army (PLA) in the last battle of the Chinese civil war and has garrisoned it ever since. The de-militarization of the island began in the early 1990s and direct contact with the mainland resumed in 2000.

Figure 1. Map of Quemoy, Taiwan, and China.

Quemoy's openings and closings

Quemoy's intertwining of border interaction and boundary security began in the fourteenth century with the combination of coastal defense and smuggling (Chiang 2011). In 1651 the retreating emperor of the Ming Dynasty, the Prince of Lu (Zhu Yihai 朱以海) took refuge there and died when the Qing conquered the island in 1663. With the opening of emigration in 1860 Quemoy residents scattered throughout Southeast Asia. By the twentieth century Quemoy, like many coastal places in Guangdong and Fujian, became dependent on remittances from overseas relatives and associations both for family welfare and major civic projects. As young people pursued their overseas opportunities Quemoy lost 40 percent of its population between 1915 and 1929 (Chiang 2011, 170). Given Fujian's history of long-distance trade and the occupation of Taiwan in 1895 by the Japanese, Quemoy's primary connections were with its mainland neighborhood and with its relatives in Southeast Asia, primarily Singapore and Hong Kong. Quemoy was occupied by the Japanese from 1937 to 1945, but it was neither a venue for development nor a frontline. Quemoy's experience with the Japanese was not the long-term transformation that Taiwan experienced, but rather like that of the rest of coastal China – brief, harsh, and military.

Previous patterns of interaction came to an abrupt end in 1949. After Quemoy was successfully defended, the ROC maintained it as a military strongpoint. At the height of tensions in the 1950s, a hundred thousand troops, one-third of the ROC's combat troops, were dug in, dodging a half-million artillery shells in the crisis of 1958. Even Secretary of State John Foster Dulles considered it "rather foolish" to station such a large force at such a distance from support and within artillery range of the mainland (*New York Times* 1958). As Tang Tsou pointed out in a contemporary analysis, Chiang Kai-shek's purpose went beyond maintaining a stepping-stone to reconquering the Mainland. He was also trying to create a casus belli between China and the United States (Tsou 1959). As Walter Lippmann put it during the 1958 crisis:

> The device that he [Chiang] is employing to entangle us is to insist…that the blockade of Quemoy can be broken only by bombarding the Mainland. But the snare for the gullible is to pretend that the Formosa air force can silence the shore batteries….What he means is that if we allow his planes to begin the attack, we with our planes would then have to take on what he has begun (Lippmann 1958)."

Quemoy was the brink of Chiang Kai-shek's brinksmanship, and the question of whether to use nuclear weapons to defend Quemoy was seriously debated in Washington. All over the world, and into the presidential debates between Kennedy and Nixon in 1960, Quemoy became a household word. The defense of Quemoy became the litmus test of steadfastness in defending the boundaries of the free world.

Meanwhile the households on Quemoy were simply battlefield extras. They were initially totally cut off from their relatives in Southeast Asia (and their remittances) as well as from the mainland (Chiang 2011). As Michael Szonyi has detailed, they were completely under military control (Szonyi 2008). For thirty years the island had twice as many soldiers as civilians, and one in five families was operating what Szonyi calls a "GI Joe business" – a small shop catering to the soldiers (Szonyi 2008). Not coincidentally, Quemoy's signature products became army-produced gaoliang (sorghum) liquor and knives made out of artillery casings. While martial law was lifted in Taiwan in 1987, the War Zone Administration remained in charge of Quemoy until 1992.

Six thousand troops remain in Quemoy in 2014, but its situation has transformed in the new century (Liu and Hsu 2014). For the first time, it is becoming a "normal" border area rather than an externally-oriented periphery or a sealed and militarized boundary. The first ferry link to Xiamen opened in January 2001 and from December 2004 Fujian residents were allowed to visit under the "mini-three links" policy. Although PRC visitors diminished when direct air links to Taiwan were opened, Quemoy remains the cheapest and most convenient point of contact. However, the PRC has developed Pingtan Island, a competing venue roughly the size of Quemoy located off the coast of Fuzhou City. The development of Pingtan into a link with Taiwan is a key part of the PRC's 2011 "Western Taiwan Strait Economic Zone," though the development of Xiamen (across from Quemoy) is also included (Chiu 2014). Meanwhile Taiwan tourists come to visit, some for army nostalgia, some to buy Mainland goods that have "floated over." And almost everyone flying back to Taipei brings a bottle of gaoliang liquor in their carry-on luggage. I did too.

Quemoy analyzed

We can lure the rich and complex texture of Quemoy back into our abstract Hegelian triad of border areas, boundaries, and horizons. As a venue of interaction, Quemoy has moved from an outward-oriented interaction with its own diaspora to a subjected and intense interaction with the military and – more distantly but directly – with the geopolitics of the Cold War. Quemoy might be called "all border area, no boundaries" before 1947, to "all boundary-edge, no border area" during the Cold War. Beyond the Cold War, Quemoy's gradient of difference is still dependent on politics. Its PRC and ROC tourists come for different reasons but the attractions derive from its border status. It is back to being a normal borderland, an area where differences meet, with boundaries creating reasons for interaction and also regulating activities.

Few places have had as intense experiences with the boundaries of governance. The Qing relaxation of emigration created a diaspora that nevertheless kept its Quemoy identity and connections. Then Battlefield Quemoy completely changed the picture. Residents were marginalized as suspect onlookers, camp followers, and occasionally as Berlin-style poster-children of freedom's heroic confrontation with tyranny. Absolute boundaries toward the mainland and even restricting relationships with relatives in Southeast Asia replaced the seaward frontier. With the thawing of ROC-PRC relations Quemoy transitioned from prominence as the experimental meeting place under the "mini-three links" to a more ordinary border situation based on the convenience of its location. Quemoy's peculiarly ambiguous status remains. It is the non-Taiwanese part of the Republic of China, and the part of Fujian Province that is not part of the People's Republic of China.

Perhaps the most interesting dimension of Quemoy's border status is that of horizons of analysis. Szonyi provides the most sustained and empathetic account in English of life on Quemoy, but as his title, *Cold War Island*, suggests, it is a life fundamentally distorted by larger frameworks. One could certainly view pre-1949 Quemoy in the context of other seaward frontier towns in Fujian and Guangdong, and its diaspora was part of the larger phenomenon of South Sea sojourners (*nanyang huaqiao*) (Wang 2003). This was a very different context from Japanese Taiwan during its fifty years of colonialism. Then with the Cold War, the few kilometers between Quemoy and the mainland became the knife edge of global confrontation, a chasm more profound than the Taiwan

Strait itself, to be defended, possibly, by general war and by nuclear weapons. The nearness of the mainland made Quemoy both the point of greatest threat of attack and the point of opportunity for Chiang's return. Meanwhile China responded to Quemoy by shelling it as the nearest bastion of its civil war enemy. Quemoy mattered so much to both sides, and to the world, that its people did not matter. The development of democracy and Taiwanese identity had resonances on Quemoy as people pressed for demilitarization, but Quemoy had never been part of Taiwan, and it did not appreciate suggestions by DPP politicians that it could be given back to the PRC (Szonyi 2008). Its new border status between Taiwan and Xiamen for the first time located the venue of international border interaction on the island itself. It became the forward foot of cross-strait contact precisely because it was on the wrong side of the Taiwan Strait. Quemoy lost its experimental status as direct contact developed between Taiwan and the Mainland but it retains its advantages of location and convenience.

Asymmetry and difference

While the first two parts of this essay concentrated on border areas as venues of difference, we now look more closely at difference itself. What is the "gradient of difference" that creates the possibility of a border venue? How do disparities on either side of the gradient affect interests, perceptions, and patterns of interaction? How is boundary governance affected by disparities in political capability? Does asymmetry relate only to national horizons, or can we analyze subnational asymmetries?

Since borderlands relate to centers, their situation is inherently asymmetric. But the typical modern border is both the venue of asymmetric contact with its center and the boundary of its own national identity in its cross-border relationship. The borderland thrives on the gradient of difference. The larger the gradient the better, as long as interaction occurs. Smuggling can be profitable for the border area precisely because it undercuts national policy (Womack 2001). If the border is transparent, then the only border advantage is international convenience. While border activity is an existential activity for its participants, it is a more abstract matter of international policy for national leadership. A border area may be more patriotic because it regularly confronts its other, but it may be less nationalistic because it depends on an active bilateral relationship. In any case, however, it is subject to the fluctuations of bilateral politics.

International differences of capabilities

For many if not most borderlands, the most important asymmetry is not the immediate one between itself and its national government, but rather the disparity between the two states that meet at the border. In the case of China's fourteen neighbors on its land border, all except Russia and India are clearly in asymmetric situations, and even these two have asymmetric aspects. But asymmetric international relationships are certainly not limited to Asia. One could consider the relationship of Mexico to the United States, or that of Guatemala to Mexico. These situations of international asymmetry are not simply matters of concern for national governments. They are particularly important for the places where the two states meet.

If two states have equal capabilities, then each can do to the other what the other can do to it. The basic calculus of the relationship should be reflexivity: the Golden Rule. If a state of roughly equal capability does something that the other does not like, it can respond in kind. However, if there is a significant disparity of capabilities then the logic of the interaction becomes more complex.

An asymmetry of capabilities exists when one side cannot do to the other what the other can do to it (Womack 2016). Even a voluntary exchange of equal values, such as normal buying and selling at the border, will be proportionally more important to the smaller side.[2] In a mutually beneficial interaction the smaller has more to gain. In an antagonistic interaction the smaller has more to lose. Thus reflexivity is not an option. If the smaller side responds in kind it will not be able to have the same effect, while the larger side has the option of raising the ante by responding with even greater capabilities. While this is most obvious in great questions of war and peace, it also affects the governance of everyday interactions as each state pursues its own interest. The larger side can bully, the smaller can resist and complain.

It might seem to be a tautology that in an asymmetric confrontation the larger side would prevail – that "might makes right." If David defeated Goliath on a regular basis then the disparity of relevant capacities would have to be recalibrated. However, in most state-to-state relationships, the capacity of the smaller side to evade and to resist should not be underestimated, and determined resistance can prevail in an asymmetric confrontation. Ironically, the mortal threat created by the capability of the larger to dominate gives the smaller the incentive for protracted resistance. By contrast, the larger side feels no mortal threat and has other policy goals that might be more important. Usually the suffering of the smaller is greater than the suffering of the larger. But the larger side can give up, while the identity of the smaller side is bound up with resistance. If identity persists despite defeat, resistance can reemerge even if the government and its army surrender. In a single interaction power will usually prevail, but over the long course of an asymmetric relationship interaction is more likely to be negotiated rather than forced.

If the resistance of the smaller can frustrate the domination of the larger, and both realize that neither can simply force the relationship, then a mature, negotiated asymmetric relationship can emerge. A negotiated asymmetric relationship is not based on equality, but it is based on mutual respect of identities. An agreement to negotiate assumes that the other side has the standing to participate in deciding the issue and that both must voluntarily commit to the outcome. Agreement implies neither unanimity nor even satisfaction with the outcome, but it does imply that remaining differences over the current transaction are less important than maintaining a normal relationship. The border then becomes a place of negotiated but still asymmetric interaction.

Not all asymmetric relationships fit the archetypal model of one state much larger in every respect than a neighboring state. There can be countervailing asymmetries, for example, China's power based on demography and Japan's based on technology. A countervailing asymmetry is not symmetry, but it is more complex than simple asymmetry. Moreover, distance between partners modifies asymmetric interactions by thinning the relationship and presenting more options to both sides. Finally, there is the question of calibrating how much disparity is necessary for a relationship to be asymmetric. But for Asia the presence of China creates a large and long set of unquestionably asymmetric relationships.

The two sides of a normal asymmetric relationship

Even in a normal asymmetric relationship, the smaller side is more exposed to the relationship than the larger, and the difference in exposure creates a difference of interest, perception, and respective behavioral patterns. The smaller has more to gain or lose in the relationship, and therefore will be more attentive to it. However, the smaller will be tempted to interpret the behavior of the larger as if the larger were equally attentive. For its part, the larger will tend to pay less attention, since it has proportionally less at play. The smaller is more alert to continuing risks and opportunities, while the larger is more concerned with moving on to more important matters. Bullying by the larger is the result both of greater capabilities and the need for closure. Allergic reactions and paranoia by the smaller reflects its greater risk.

The systemic error of asymmetric relationships may be laid at the feet of the Golden Rule. The larger views the smaller as a smaller version of itself – itself minus the capabilities – and therefore of little interest unless it allies with powers of greater capabilities. The smaller views the larger as itself magnified – therefore very scary, because it is just as interested and has the power. In fact, what the smaller needs in the relationship is exactly what the larger does not need – reassurance that its identity and interests are respected. What the larger needs is what the smaller cannot imagine for itself – deference for its larger capabilities and assurance that the smaller is not scheming to reverse the relationship. In a normal asymmetric relationship, the exchange of deference for acknowledgment of identity is the key to stability.

If we take the relationship of China and Vietnam as an archetypal example of an asymmetric relationship, we can see the effects of asymmetry at both the national level and at the border (Womack 2006). At the national level, the relationship is not simply a matter of the diplomacy of the two governments, but rather of attitudes shared by the entire political communities. Vietnamese are more worried about China than the Chinese are about Vietnam. At the border, Chinese merchants see Vietnam as an extension of their domestic markets and as inexpensive opportunities for international tourism, while Vietnamese are more purchasers and hosts to tourism. The differences between the states create opportunities at the border, and these opportunities are shaped by asymmetry.

Quemoy as a prism of asymmetry

At first glance Quemoy might seem to be proof that might makes right. The Convention of Beijing of 1860 forced the Qing government to abandon its emigration restrictions, launching Quemoyans into the South China Sea. The defeat of the KMT on the mainland threatened Quemoy, but the intervention of the US Navy in 1950 added a heavy foot to Taiwan's side of the scale. When that foot was lifted in 1979 the shift in the balance of power created a Taiwan fearfully cooperative with the Mainland and Quemoy briefly became the fulcrum of the shift.

But asymmetry is much more complicated than disequilibrium and its shifts. Clearly the defeat and downfall of the Qing did not quench the identity of China or its desire to regain its autonomy. Defeat by Western imperialism was real, and its effect on coastal China was especially profound. In 1895 the link between Fujian and Taiwan was broken by the Treaty of Shimonoseki, but the broader web of Quemoy's diaspora to the South China Sea became more important. However, humiliation also engendered China's modern politics, leading ultimately to the civil war that reversed Quemoy's fate by breaking its link to the near shore and linking its fate to Taiwan more strongly than ever before. Quemoy became the symbol of the civil war's contested conclusion. As the PRC shifted its policy to peaceful reunification and the Taiwanese found their political voice the situation of Quemoy became more complex: a border governed by a distant island.

Quemoy is no longer protected by the United States, or for that matter by Taiwan, despite the continuing presence of troops. Its security lies not in military defenses, but rather in the political habituation of both the PRC and ROC to peaceful relations and in the hope that it can prosper as their meeting place (as a matter of the low politics of convenience rather than the high politics of negotiation). Quemoy remains at the intersection of two planes of dynamic asymmetric relationships, the national one between the PRC and the ROC and the subnational one of Taiwan and its most prominent non-Taiwanese part.

Quemoy is certainly out of step with recent political trends in Taiwan. In the January 2016 presidential election the KMT candidate, Eric Chu, received 66 percent of the Quemoy vote, twice the Taiwan percentage, and the DPP winner, Tsai Ing-wen, received 18 percent, one-third of her Taiwan share. It is likely that the combination of Quemoy's special association with the army and its vital interest in smooth relations with the Mainland were factors in the voting. In any case, it is unlikely that the DPP will feel obliged to pay much attention to Quemoy's special border relationship.

Quemoy's asymmetric relationship to the Mainland is less predictable. Cross-Strait tensions are likely to rise during Tsai Ing-wen's administration, but they are not likely to deteriorate into hostility. After all, it was her DPP predecessor, Chen Shui-bian, who initiated the mini-three links policy in 2001. Perhaps if direct cross-Strait exchange became more constrained, Quemoy could once again become a special venue as a permitted point of contact. Such developments are of course unpredictable, but the rationale of the speculation illustrates the located and asymmetric interests of borderlands.

Notes

1. The terms "thesis, antithesis, synthesis" are often misattributed to Hegel, but in fact he never used the terms, although Fichte, his predecessor at University of Berlin, did. Nevertheless, Hegel's whole philosophical system is structured in triads of moments which are aggregated into ever larger triads. The first moment expresses the positive essence of an idea, the second expresses its limitations, which can be its practical expressions. The third expresses the underlying harmony of its essence and definition. See G.W.F. Hegel, *Enzyklopädie der philosophischen Wissenschaften*, 3rd edn., passim.
2. "Larger" and "smaller" should be understood in terms of the relevant disparity of capabilities.

References

Chan, Yuk Wah. 2013. *Vietnamese-Chinese Relationships at the Borderlands: Trade, Tourism, and Cultural Practices*. New York: Routledge.

Chiang, Bo-wei. 2011. "A Special Intermittance and Continuity in Local History: The Chinese Diaspora and Their Hometown in Battlefield Quemoy during 1949-1960s." *Journal of Chinese Overseas* 7: 169–186.

Chiu, Chui-Cheng. 2014. "Observing China's Strategy and Policy of Sub-regional Cooperation Toward Taiwan." Paper presented at The Rise of China and the Tangled Development in East Asia conference at Quemoy University, October 24–25.

Lippmann, Walter. 1958. "A Mediator is Needed." *New York Herald Tribune* September 23.

Liu, Pei-Yi, and Shu-Ming Hsu. 2014. "An Analysis of Strategic Value and Positioning Adjustment in Kinmen." Paper presented at The Rise of China and the Tangled Development in East Asia conference at Quemoy University, October 24–25.

New York Times. 1958. "State Department Transcript of Remarks Made by Dulles at News Conference." October 1.

Scott, James C. 2009. *The Art of Not Being Governed: An Anarchist History of Upland Southeast Asia*. New Haven, CT: Yale University Press.

Skinner, G. William. 1977. "Urban Development in Imperial China." *The City in Late Imperial China*, 3–32. Palo Alto, CA: Stanford University Press.

Szonyi, Michael. 2008. *Cold War Island*. New York: Cambridge University Press.

Tsou, Tang. 1959. *The Embroilment over Quemoy: Mao, Chiang, and Dulles*, University of Utah Institute of International Studies International Study Paper no. 2.

Wang, Gungwu. 2003. *China and The Chinese Overseas*. Singapore: Eastern Universities Press.

Womack, Brantly. 2001. "China's Border Trade and Its Relationship to the National Political Economy." *The American Asian Review* 19 (2): 31–48.

Womack, Brantly. 2006. *China and Vietnam: The Politics of Asymmetry*. New York: Cambridge University Press.

Womack, Brantly. 2016. *Asymmetry and International Relationships*. New York: Cambridge University Press.

Mobile North Korean women and their places in the Sino-North Korea borderland[†]

Sung Kyung Kim

This article explores the situations of people living at the China-North Korea borderland. Contrary to the general understanding of North Korean migrants – as victims of the North Korean brutal state and economic impoverishment – many North Koreans at the Sino-North Korea borderland cross the border (a border river) as a matter of everyday practice. This article thus contests the general restrictive stereotypes that frame North Korean mobility, and argues that many of them are calculative agents actively balancing the costs and benefits of migration. A decision of migration often takes into account North Koreans' spatial perception, intimate human network of relatives, and sense of familiarity with language, feelings and emotions for place and people, with little reference to the political persecution or economic deprivation usually depicted by the media.

Introduction

North Korean mobility tends to be narrowly framed in relation to either brutal state violations or severe economic crisis, the so-called "Arduous March" (1995–1998) (Aldrich 2011).[1] Within this frame, North Korean migrants are understood as mere victims of the North Korean regime as well as of unprecedented economic crisis, and subsequently the agency of North Korean migrants is to a great extent underestimated (Kim 2012). It seems that, increasingly, North Korean migrants actively pursue a better life and this allows them to be selective in their choice of destinations and places of settlement. More importantly, the majority may not even have intended to "migrate" to "foreign countries" in the beginning, but rather were merely "coming and going across the river like going to a neighbouring village and did not express serious concern about crossing the border" (Korean Human Rights Commission 2009, 69). North Korean border-crossers tend to share familiar feelings and sensibilities in the Sino-North Korea borderland, so that the border-crossing act itself does not suggest to them that they are actually "crossing the national border." Moreover, transnational communities in the borderland, including Korean Chinese, South Koreans, and North Korean border-crossers, seem to offer a certain level of intimacy that attracts more North Korean migrants to cross the river. Given these diverse factors behind North Korean mobility, this article argues for more nuanced approaches towards North Korean mobility in the Sino-North Korea

---

[†] A part of this article has appeared in a previous publication in Korean by the author. In this article, the author has added new research materials and revised the theoretical framework.

borderland. In particular, I maintain that North Korean mobility becomes possible as a result of not only the migrants' rational calculation of cost-benefit, but also, and perhaps more importantly, their shared feelings and sensibilities constructed within history and culture. This article thus critically deconstructs the current stereotypes of North Korean mobility and argues that North Korean's shared feelings and senses directly link to the numerous instances of their border-crossing.

Migration has been mainly framed in terms of economic rationality, especially in neoclassical and even new economic approaches.[2] Migrants as rational beings actualize their desires and aspirations "to 'better' themselves in material respects" via facilitating their rationality and calculating the cost-benefit of their migration (Massey et al. 1993; Ravenstein 1889, 289). Neoclassical and new economic approaches have often been criticized on the grounds that they downplay non-economic factors such as emotions, affects, and sentiments. The cost-benefit perspective on migration may be useful to explain the instrumental reasons behind mobility, including push-pull factors on a more structural level, but may not be able to account for those who decide not to migrate or to return to their homeland even though it does not provide the same economic opportunities as foreign countries. In particular, the case of North Korean mobility cannot entirely fit into an economic value-oriented framework.

Indeed, non-rational factors have often been ignored in attempts to understand human action. In response to this, much recent anthropological research has dealt with irrational elements that actually generate mobility and transnational connections, such as intimacy, emotional attachments and the will for a better life (Chu 2010; Gamburd 2000; Kwon 2015). In line with this previous research, this article introduces spatial perceptions, senses of familiarity with language, landscapes, everyday lives, and intimate networks of relatives, all of which stand as core components that contribute to the decision-making processes among North Korean migrants. I also argue that these sensibilities, feelings, and emotions are historically and spatially embedded, so that North Korean residents in the Sino-North Korea borderland are particularly active in their border crossing.

It is hard to estimate the exact number of North Korean border-crossers, but it is fair to say that millions of North Koreans have been crossing the border since the mid-1990s. Most North Koreans move back and forth between China and North Korea rather than fleeing to South Korea or any other country, and approximately 50,000~100,000 North Koreans have settled on the Chinese side of the borderland despite their illegal status. Some North Koreans have arrived in South Korea, with the number totalling 28,795 from 1953 until 2015. A high proportion of females make up this flow to the South, approximately 70 per cent of the total, with those originating from North Hamgyong Province – the northernmost province of North Korea – estimated at roughly 63 per cent (Ministry of Unification 2016). North Koreans settling on the Chinese side of the borderland are also mostly women, the majority of whom also have originated from North Hamgyong Province. It is thus reasonable to argue that mobility, even of North Korean women going to South Korea, is closely related to the Sino-North Korea borderland and its cultural and historical resources.

This article is based on ethnographic research data. I worked as a volunteer social worker during 2011–2013 and my role was to help two North Korean families settle in South Korea. I additionally interviewed 20 North Koreans settling in South Korea as a result of applying a snowball sampling method in 2013–2015. I also undertook field research in the Sino-North Korea borderland during the summers of 2011, 2012, and 2015. During the field research in China, I interviewed five South Korean missionaries, three ethnic Korean missionaries, three South Korean businessmen, one ethnic Korean businessman, two South Korean human rights activists, and two North Korean government officials. All interviews were audio-recorded and transcribed except for one, as one North Korean government official refused to be recorded.

The Sino-North Korea borderland

Most of the northern border of North Korea is adjacent to China and is 1,416 km long (Pinilla 2004, 2).[3] The border with Russia is at the mouth of the Tumen River and is only 16.93 km wide. In 1964, North Korea and China, in a protocol concerning mutual cooperation on work to maintain national security and social order in the borderland area, described the borderland as "a city, county, prefecture that adjoins the two countries" (O. Lee 2011, 18). As such, this region has continuously conducted economic exchanges, both informally and formally, with China and Russia, and its geographical division (consisting of a river) serves as an advantage as it minimizes the cost of such exchanges. It is a borderland, both socially and geographically (Takamura 2004, 174–175; Vaughan-Williams 2009).

In a global sense, the territory of many modern states was fixed at the beginning of the twentieth century. Since then the symbolic, political, and geographical border has represented important standards in constructing differences from the "other." The border is formed based on the institutionalisation or production of the modern state's territory and is a modern product (Newman and Paasi 1998). At times, the established border functions unilaterally, without considering communities that have set down their roots in the region. For this reason, irregularities exist in the belief that "the border" is "clearly" political and economic, and there are many instances where the border drawn on the map has not operated in a unified manner in day-to-day life (Balibar 1998). In reality, state and territory are often not clearly divided and the boundary works in alternative ways.

Horstmann, while stressing the dynamism of the borderland, asserts that the narrative underpinning different regions may function in two different layers. First there is the layer where the political sovereignty of the state and the border functions. Second there is the space created by the people who live in the borderland (Horstmann 2002, 7). The borderland, which is itself divided by the border, may have more frequent linkages denoting a regional and cultural sense of kinship specific to the borderland than cultural ties with the state to which it belongs. For this reason, rather than understanding the borderland as two states adjacent to each other and centered on the border, it may better be understood as a common social space where people have established their dwelling; in other words, a "common place" for a "common people" (Baud and Schendel 1997, 216; Brednikova and Voronkov 2000). Moreover, rather than being the "other" region, the borderland may overcome foreignness and borders, and is a region formed by various exchanges and actors (Wendle and Rosler 1999, 8). The borderland, an everyday space very often created before the modern border was established, maintains communities at a level different from that of a formal division or obstacle. If people of the same ethnicity, or who speak the same language, dwell in this area, the modern territory's boundary, known as the border, is yet another everyday space and can function powerfully in that regard.

The aforementioned characteristics of borderlands can be found in the North Hamgyong Province of North Korea and the Yanbian Korean Autonomous Prefecture, where official space and everyday place intersect in a dynamic manner. In the nineteenth century, even after the modern border was established, ethnic Koreans in China and North Koreans maintained the borderland characteristic of being connected by blood ties, language, ethnicity, and culture. The approximately two million ethnic Koreans in China have resided collectively in the borderland and retain the Korean language and culture with the support of China's policy for minority ethnicities. Since the formation of the two modern states, the political sovereignties of both via border control, including treaties, policies and institutions, clearly operate as well.

However, everyday lives in the Sino-North Korea borderland also incapacitate border control in official space. The smuggling business is a good example. As the Tumen River is the border between the two states, technically the river is common space for both. Chinese, normally ethnic Korean, and North Korean smugglers use boats to get closer to the other side, but they do not anchor to the land but instead throw their wares to the nearby banks. In doing so, none of the smugglers actually violate border control rules. Furthermore, smugglers tend to construct informal networks with border guards through bribery so that smuggling across the border has to some extent become protected by official power. One of my interviewees, a 28-year-old male now living in South Korea, used to be involved in the smuggling business when he was in North Korea. His main product was gold, which was light enough to throw from the boat. He normally took his boat across the river very early in the morning, around 5 am, after secretly obtaining the permission of North Korean border guards. He then approached the Chinese side, getting as close as possible so that he could throw the gold or other wares to his business partners, who were waiting for him on the river bank:

> Providing that we do not approach the land, we are fine. As long as we are floating in the river, it's okay.... Then, normally we get close and then throw it. My business partner [*daebang* in North Korean] in China was waiting there to collect it [gold]

Residents in the borderland use diverse methods to maintain their connections and networks which might cause ruptures in the strict rules of official spaces for everyday exchanges. The river itself is common space for both North Korea and China, so that North Korean smugglers and their Chinese, mostly ethnic Korean counterparts actively use this unique characteristic of the borderland in their business.

Mobile North Koreans and their spatial perception in the borderland

Given the particular characteristics of the Sino-North Korea borderland, there have long been frequent and temporary migrations among ethnic Koreans and North Koreans. Before the economic crisis in North Korea, migration flows appear to have been unidirectional from China to North Korea and undertaken by ethnic Koreans (Smith in NKIDP e-dossiers 2012, 1). From the late 1950s to the end of the 1970s, ethnic Koreans legally and illegally migrated to North Korea from China in order to escape economic difficulties and racial discrimination, with the North Korean government offering housing, food, money and work to returnees as it needed labor power for cooperative farms and factories. I interviewed one woman in China, 72 years old in 2012, who portrays this type of mobility. Born in Najin, North Korea, close to the borderland, her parents migrated to the northeast region of China with her when she was a toddler. After completing her education, she got married and migrated back to North Korea at the beginning of the 1960s. She occasionally visited China to meet her brothers, and migrated to China once again soon after her husband passed away. Her brothers are well settled in China and her extended relatives have been helping her to stay in China.

The poor economic conditions of ethnic Koreans in China caused them to permanently migrate to North Korea or to temporarily visit relatives there to gain economic assistance and make exchanges. Official Chinese documents clearly state that the outflow of ethnic Koreans was caused by economic difficulties in northeastern China (NKIDP e-dossiers 2012). In order to resolve this issue, the Chinese government attempted to improve food supplies and to strengthen ideological education. In addition, the Chinese government legalized those "border residents who had proper reasons to visit relatives in or travel to [North] Korea" for mobility in order to encourage them to return (NKIDP e-dossiers 2012, 13). Despite the concerns of the Chinese government, the outflows of ethnic Korean continued legally and illegally until the end of the 1970s; this traffic played a crucial role in sustaining everyday connections among ethnic and North Koreans. The mobility of ethnic Koreans produced certain shared sentiments among residents in the borderland, which in turn encouraged further migration flows from North Korea to China during the 1990s and 2000s.

The majority of the Koreans who migrated north of the Tumen River are from North Hamgyong Province. After their migration, these Koreans continued to carry out everyday exchanges and maintain blood relations with the North Hamgyong Province residents (H. Lee et al. 2006, 14). Until the early 1980s, many ethnic Koreans in China crossed the border into North Korea to sell goods and buy North Korea's minerals and food products. Such exchanges served as the foundation for ethnic Koreans in China and North Koreans to maintain blood relations. Subsequently, as the North Korean economic crisis became severe, the situation reversed and the North Koreans began to seek the help of the ethnic Koreans in China (Kim 2012). Thus the ethnic Koreans in China and the North Hamgyong Province residents, on the basis of blood ties from the past, created a unique everyday space. This space is a type of "cultural and linguistic zone" on the basis of a shared culture and language (Kim 2012). Those North Korean border-crossers who migrated during the economic crisis should not be generalized as people "who turned their backs on their countries and crossed the border." Rather, they should be investigated in terms of the everyday space of the border-crossers and the ethnic Koreans in China that was built over a long period.

Since 1992, the borderland entered a period of reconstruction with the influx of South Korean migrants; this is when South Korea and China established diplomatic relations. Informal human networks between the two countries have become legalized and intensified, taking on diplomatic relations as well as Chinese economic reform. Thousands of ethnic Koreans who became economic migrants moved to South Korea, and similar numbers of South Koreans have also migrated to China. The number of Koreans in China has reached 2,573,928 and the number of South Korean migrants in China was 350,529 in 2013 (Ministry of Foreign Affair 2014). Some 64 percent of ethnic Koreans are concentrated in three northeastern provinces in China, Liaoning, Jilin and Heilongjiang, (Koo 2011, 2013). Foreign companies in the Yanbian Korean Autonomous Prefecture number 634, and of these 448 are South Korean, clearly requiring significant numbers of South Korean migrants (*Inminnet*, December 19, 2013). Clearly, the Sino-North Korea borderland has undergone rapid change in its dynamics due to the influx of capital and people from South Korea. In addition, a significant number of ethnic Koreans have returned to the borderland with new capital and networks after spending years in South Korea. South Korean lifestyles via formal and informal networks between South Korea and China have become widespread in the borderland, and this makes the Sino-North Korea borderland a hybrid transnational space. Fashion items and popular culture from South Korea simultaneously became widespread in Yanbian.

Thousands of South Korean migrants, as well as tourists, have led to the flourishing of a leisure and service industry targeting them in the borderland. Indeed, the Sino-North Korean borderland implies not only border culture between China and North Korea, but also transnational communities of Koreans.

Given this dynamism in the borderland, North Koreans there have managed to become involved in both legal and illegal mobility. Legal visitors can normally get a three month permit from the North Korean government if they can prove they have relatives in China. Obtaining permission to visit China requires at least two hundred dollars as bribery, so North Korean border-crossers attempt to stay longer than three months in order to earn sufficient money or benefits from relatives.[4] Thus, legal visitors seem to become illegal migrants easily, but the North Korean government does not seem to restrict them from staying in China, since they actively bring in capital to North Korea. Most legal migrants rely on their blood ties, ethnic Koreans, for finding jobs and other economic benefits. Because of the influx of South Korean migrants and capital, cooperation between South Koreans and ethnic Chinese has skyrocketed in the borderland, which implies North Korean migrants linking to South Koreans via ethnic Chinese.

In recent years, more and more legal North Korean workers with one-year contracts have come to China to work in factories and restaurants (Demick 2012). In Dandong in China, approximately 30,000 legal workers have been reported.[5] Most of them, carefully selected by the North Korean government, come from Pyongyang, and tend to work up to 14 hours a day in inadequate working conditions. Legal contract workers in Yanji, the biggest city in Yanbian Autonomous Prefecture, are fewer than in Dandong, but have increased from 1500 to 3000 (*Yanhap News*, July, 30, 2014). In addition, around 20,000 North Korean legal workers are in Russia, with 3000 of them in Vladivostok (Y. Lee 2012, 60–61). Legal workers in both countries are tightly controlled by the North Korean state political security department, and tend to prefer to return to their homeland after earning money.[6] These legal workers may not have much freedom to meet ethnic Chinese or South Koreans because of tight control, but they are more exposed to the consumer culture that has been rapidly developed in the borderland. In this sense, they become the bearers of consumer culture and capitalistic knowledge, and may bring significant changes to North Korea in the long term.

During the Arduous March, most border-crossers had little intention to stay in China or migrate to South Korea; in North Hamgyong Province, North Korean residents have perceived the borderland as their everyday place. National border and border control as restrictions on mobility were tenuous for a long time, and North Korean residents and ethnic Koreans in the borderland had strong connections and networks. Examples of their experiences include living in China for a considerable period and migrating back to North Korea, exchanging goods over the Tumen River with ethnic Koreans in China, visits from ethnic Korean relatives in China, ethnic Korean peddlers coming to the village, North Koreans going to China for business and, in the case of young children, swimming and playing with ethnic Koreans in the Tumen River. Drawing from their lifeworld-embedded historical experiences and memories, many North Korean residents in the borderland planned and went through with crossing the border.

I interviewed one young man who migrated to South Korea in 2007, who originated in North Hamgyong Province and spent 11 years in China. During his stay in China he was involved in the smuggling business with North Koreans and therefore travelled back and forth to North Korea. He said that those who are not familiar with the culture of the borderland would not be able to even think about crossing the river:

Everything is ultimately the riverside. People from other provinces do not even think about coming. Maybe people who go to North Hamgyong Province for business may think about it. People on the riverside are very knowledgeable. They always cross over. They know it all. They have ears and eyes, so how can they not know?

The North Korean regime has restricted people's mobility domestically; North Korean residents require travel permission from the government and most live in government-designated areas (J. Seo 2005). One of the characteristics of North Korean society is the control over people's mobility, and information and knowledge is heavily censored by the government. Because of this, even during the worst famine, most North Koreans did not even think about crossing the border, and only residents in the borderland moved to China. As interviews indicate, only a very few people from Hwanghae and Kangwon Provinces, far from the border, could even come up with the idea of crossing the border.

The world of North Koreans living in more outlying regions of the country goes beyond this, enabling them to go beyond the border to build relationships and connect with ethnic Korean communities in China. When the economic crisis intensified, it was plausible for residents of the borderland to cross over into China and attain economic profit, rather than moving to other areas within North Korea or seeking help from relatives in Pyongyang. One older woman described her own decision to migrate to China:

…[my husband had] liver cancer, and my son suddenly came back from the army due to malnutrition. My husband died, and I had to find a way to save my son. I don't know why, but I could not even imagine contacting my brother to ask for help. He was in Pyongyang in a high position. The only thing in my mind was "crossing the river."

Those people who are disconnected or excluded in North Korean society may arrive at the idea of relocating themselves to China more easily. I interviewed a 46-year-old woman from North Hamgyong Province who arrived in South Korea in 2014 after spending 10 years moving back and forth between China and North Korea. She had had a hard life as her father was accused of being a political offender. When her father disappeared, she realized that the entire family was stigmatized as traitors. Because of this, her marriage did not go well, and she had to find a way to survive with her young son. The only option for her was to cross the border:

[After the disappearance of my father] we realized that our documents clearly indicated that we were the family of a political traitor. All my sisters and brothers had given up their social lives by then. Although we were doing well at school, we did not have any hope to become members of the party. There was nothing else I could do. I crossed the border.

The feminization of North Korean mobility

A distinct feature of the migration of North Korean border-crossers is that 70 per cent are women. Women made up 12.2 percent of migrants during the period when the number of border-crossers was relatively low (1948–1998). Those that crossed the border to the south subsequent to the Korean War were primarily male soldiers or government bureaucrats, and these gender ratios continued until after the mid-1990s. However, beginning in 1998, the number of women border-crossers increased exponentially. After reaching a majority in 2002, the percentage grew larger and has remained at 70 percent for the past several years (Ministry of Unification 2016).

These figures demonstrate that the migration of North Korean border-crossers has become gendered. Hence, there is a need to reinvestigate the Sino-North Korea borderland, which is the initial space in which they reside, within the gendered relationship of the space/place framework. Space and place is a specific cultural structure of gender and a location for gender relationships (Massey 1999, 177). Structured space and place exert important influences on the way gender is constructed and understood in society. Moreover, according to the constitution of social relationships, space and place can be perceived and experienced differently by each actor. The Sino-North Korea borderland is a place that is complicatedly entwined with global capitalism, a transnational ethnic economy, and the patriarchal gender relationships that make such processes possible.

The migration of North Koreans within the Sino-North Korea borderland is closely connected to social changes among ethnic Koreans in China. Up until the 1990s, China's policy restricted the movement of residents in each of its regions. For this reason, 97 percent of all ethnic Koreans in China in this earlier era resided in the three northeastern provinces of China (Kwon and Park 2004, 538). However, once diplomatic relations were established in 1992 between South Korea and China, economic exchanges between the two countries increased exponentially. After many ethnic Koreans in China left for South Korea for economic migration, the gap provided sufficient space for North Korean border-crossers to migrate to China. The trend of ethnic Koreans in China migrating to South Korea, which became full-fledged in the mid- to late-1990s, illustrates a distinct feature of global economic migration, that is, the feminization of migration. Because of the expansion of the service industry in South Korea, the increase in demand for household help, nannies, and caregivers due to more South Korean women entering the workforce, and South Korean women's growing tendency to avoid marriage, increasing numbers of female ethnic Koreans from China migrated to South Korea (Lee et al. 2006, 259; Sassen 1991).

North Korean women filled the gap left by the women who migrated to South Korea. If the ethnic Korean women from China filled the gap for "female" jobs avoided by women in South Korea, it was the North Korean women with illegal statuses working for a lower wage and enduring all sorts of injustices who filled the gap in China. This illustrates the "reproduction of the international division of labour," where a structure of inequality functions within the global economic system (Lee et al. 2006; Sassen 1991).

However, the reason why the number of North Korean women who migrated to China is far larger than the number of men is not only due to the gap left by ethnic Korean women in China. If the North Korean economic crisis, which began in the mid-1990s, led many women to become agents of informal economic activities centered on the marketplace, such as smuggling goods, men often remained in the jobs given to them by the North Korean authorities. The Arduous March demolished parts of the social control system in North Korea, but male labor concentrated in major government-owned industry, especially heavy industry, was still subject to the government's tight control. On the other hand, female labor was concentrated in light or service industries, so they could have more freedom from government control. In this sense, North Korean women became the main agents for household economy, and they have started to engage in various market activities including not just smuggling, but also trading and sales. By doing these, their life-worlds becomes much wider, extending beyond the national border, and the borderland perceived by North Korean women in the market has been dynamically reconstructed. They have indeed become mobile subjects.

Life experiences of North Korean women in the borderland

For these mobile North Korean women, the situation on the Chinese side of the borderland has been tough. Engaging with the informal economic domain rather than carrying out formal economic activities, due to their illegal status, the North Korean women must deal with unjust treatment or live in hiding in country villages to avoid notice by public security. The spaces to construct the perception of place for North Korean women display a gendered personality more confining and unequal than that for their male North Korean counterparts. If North Korean men are able to reside in the city or farm village as part of the lowest working class, North Korean women usually live in spaces where they are seen as "women with illegal status." North Korean women in China can be divided into those marrying ethnic Koreans in China or Han Chinese in the agricultural regions and serving the patriarchal system, and those working in restaurants, massage shops, or bars in the city or engaging in the sex industry. Although these two groups settle in different social spaces, both groups exist within a capitalist market intimately connected with patriarchy.

The North Korean women who settle down in the agricultural regions play the roles of mother, wife, and daughter-in-law within the patriarchal system in place of the ethnic Korean women who had migrated to South Korea or to large cities in China. As one ethnic Korean woman in China told me,

> My brother was unable to get married. There isn't anyone who wants to live in the countryside farming and he was living all alone even at age 40. Then one morning, my mother found a North Korean woman collapsed in the front yard. Out of sympathy, [my mother] allowed her to live there and she ended up living with my brother. They lived together for over a year, but then she ran away. My brother looked very pitiful. So, upon hearing about a good North Korean woman, we paid some money and brought her here. We paid 2000 won.

This sort of phenomenon demonstrates the significance of the role of North Korean women in sustaining farming regions in the Sino-North Korea borderland. Here, the North Korean women take on the tasks of childbirth, household labor, farming, and taking care of parents. Many women refuse to play these roles today; but these women adaptively accept the unequal relationships inherent in this patriarchal system because of their illegal status. In the case of women who have crossed the border numerous times or have experienced forced repatriation, they seek a stable space for residence. Since the farming village is some distance from the city, this place of dwelling becomes a relatively safe space.

One ethnic Korean woman I interviewd first began to cross the border in 1997 and went back and forth between North Korea and China on numerous occasions. She managed to live in China over 10 years, but she was repatriated to North Korea in 2008. After being imprisoned, she escaped North Korea again and then migrated to South Korea in 2014. As she told me,

> We don't have other ways to survive in China. Our kind of people live in very similar ways. Working in restaurants. ... Of course I got a man. I was not trafficked. I know that our kind of people are often trafficked for marriage. I knew one ethnic Korean woman. I told her that you could sell me, but I would like to meet a man first. I kept telling her that I would live here so you should bring someone I could really live with. She was good to me. She brought the man, ethnic Korean. He was very diligent.

She understands very well that illegal North Korean women need a safety net, which normally refers to legal Chinese (ethnic Korean or Han) men. She engineered her relationship to ensure successful settlement in China with a young child. She thus actively used marriage to a Chinese man in order to secure her safety and settle down in China. This sense of volition has been commonly overlooked, with such experiences described as human trafficking. But some North Korean women often understand this "human trafficking" in a different context. Within particular sets of constraints, some of them actively facilitate relationships or marriage with Chinese men as a means of settlement in China.

Of course, a considerable number of North Korean women are indeed sold as marriage migrants into agricultural regions through human trafficking. During this process, women may experience extensive sexual assault and infringement of their human rights (Lee H. 2011). North Korean women who are trafficked by brokers are exposed to a blind spot within human rights, as they are being bought and sold as the lowest class in Chinese society and treated as sex that is being traded.

Despite the human rights problems experienced by the North Korean women, they may slowly begin to make meaning of the space they live in and attempt in various ways to settle down. This is illustrated by another woman I interviewed, who first began to cross the border in 1997 and went back and forth between North Korea and China on numerous occasions. She married in 2004 and settled down in a farming village in the Yanbian region. Even while working at a restaurant, she was always apprehensive due to her illegal status. She decided that marrying and settling down in a countryside village would be better and so chose to migrate out to the country:

> People told me that I should marry into a farming village rather than wandering around, and that way I would be able to live… I found my husband's house and went in but, oh my, this so-called house was a thatched cottage. But as soon as I stepped foot into the house, my heart felt comfortable and at ease. There was no sense of unfamiliarity; I felt like it was my home. After that, I had to adapt to the people there. There is a big difference between people in the farming village and those in the city. Farming people are very ignorant. Most of the people are culturally and intellectually no higher than those who don't graduate from primary school. After going in there, I became, in one word, their coordinator. I would drag people here and there doing everything for them. I would take them to karaoke since I was in Yanji for four or five years; I helped them all. I took them to the market and helped them buy things.

She had attended college in North Korea, but had to fulfil tasks that were completely new to her, such as farm work, while taking care of her husband. She never considered migrating to South Korea; the farming village was already evolving into a place for her to live. A major reason for her satisfaction is that the farming village is located in the borderland area, making possible various forms of communication with North Korea. She left a daughter in North Korea; her husband, who is an ethnic Korean, visits her daughter in North Korea regularly to provide money and deliver needed goods. Moreover, upon being able to speak on a regular basis with her daughter using the mobile phone that was delivered to her daughter, she experienced no dissatisfaction with being a farmer's wife in the countryside, which made all these developments possible.

There are a considerable number of women who migrate to South Korea after experiencing discord with their husbands or being unable to adapt to life in a farming village after marriage migration (Cho 2011; Korean Human Rights Commission 2009; Lee, H. 2011). In particular, there are frequent occurrences of North Koreans running away after marrying a Han Chinese farmer and experiencing the language barrier or a sense of repulsion at engaging in conjugal relations, as this is a purchase marriage. For example, one woman I interviewed was sold to a family in Hubei Province and maintained her marriage for eight years with an old Han Chinese man; she experienced severe migraines due to continued stress:

> Because they are a different ethnicity, there is no sense of comfort. I can't have any form of communication. There was so much conflict. Even after suppressing myself, it accumulates and accumulates and the headaches I already had, my headaches were so painful I couldn't drink water, or eat, and I would throw up. So if it hurt too much I would even try hitting my head.

North Korean women who engaged in marriage migration to the ethnic Korean farm villages in China experienced less difference in language and culture and had an easier experience of adapting. But on the other hand, some research has found that North Korean women prefer Han Chinese husbands, as they displayed a less patriarchal attitude compared to ethnic Korean or North Korean men (Lee, H. 2011, 389–391). Another woman I interviewed married a Han farmer and gave birth to a son and lived in China for seven years. She was talented in dancing and singing, enough to have actively participated in an art troupe in North Korea; she eventually decided that rather than living in China doing farm work, her life would be better if she migrated to South Korea.

> There's no end to the work. My husband treated me well, and there isn't anyone as nice as him, but imagining the rest of my life just working like that was too terrible. Even now, my husband will call me and cry, asking me to come back...

She had had quite a difficult time adopting the role of mother as well as farmer's wife. Sometimes, unable to adapt to their life, North Korean women like her leave their farming life to migrate to other cities within China or South Korea.

The migration of Koreans into China was a primary reason for the migration of ethnic Koreans in China to cities. As Korean companies began to move into the coastal regions of China after its opening in 1992, there was an increasing need for a Korean-speaking labor force of ethnic Koreans in China. Following the influx of Koreans, the ethnic Koreans in China began to move away from the farming areas of the three northeastern provinces, which had functioned as their settlement, to move into the cities of the three northeastern provinces, to major cities like Beijing or Shanghai, or to cities in the coastal regions (Chengdu, Weihai, Yantai) which allowed access to South Korea by ship (Kwon and Park 2004, 65).

Korean companies maintained close relationships with ethnic Koreans when expanding into China. While analyzing the relationship with Koreans and ethnic Koreans in China, particularly with the structure of "Korean = employer, ethnic Korean = employee" or "Korean = investor, ethnic Korean = intermediary," Chun and Huh argue that in Korean enterprises in China, the community of Koreans, ethnic Koreans, and Han Chinese live in symbiosis (Chun and Huh 2004, 296–352 cited in Koo 2011, 425). As Koreans emerged as new subjects for economic and cultural exchanges, not only did the ethnic Korean society in China quickly transform, but the North Koreans who crossed the border also transformed (Kim 2012).

Even now, a large number of North Koreans continue to move anywhere that may seem safe. Obviously, North Koreans with illegal statuses, as well as border-crossers, are positioned at the lowest rank of the labor force within the transnational ethnic space and are engaged in the occupational category of intensive labor avoided by ethnic Koreans in China, care-taking work, or service work, meeting the economic and lifestyle needs of ethnic Koreans and Korean nationals. In this sense, the Sino-North Korea borderland, where the ethnic Koreans in China and North Koreans met and carried out exchanges over a long period, did not remain in the geopolitical borderland but expanded into the large cities of China. The experience of women is quite distinct from that of men. If North Korean men usually earn a living through simple labor, it is common for North Korean women to engage in adult entertainment establishments or in the sex industry. The increasing demand for service industry work following the migration of Korean companies and independent businessmen has generated much greater demand for migrant women.

The problem is that, for North Korean women with an illegal status, in a more constraining environment than that in which ethnic Korean women find themselves in China, the range of choice for occupations is inevitably much more restrictive. Women are flowing into the sex industry through various channels; cases have been heard of North Korean women believing they would be working in a restaurant and getting turned over to the sex industry upon crossing the border, while other women who are unable to endure farm work escape to the large cities and have to enter into prostitution (Korean Human Rights Commission 2009). For women who have stayed in China for a longer time, it is understood that they have either married a Chinese (ethnic Korean in China or Han Chinese) or have worked in a service job. As one informant told me of one of her acquaintances,

> Did she get married in China?... By the look of it, it seems like she is working in one of those places [in the sex industry] in China. Of the North Korean women, if they didn't get married in China or didn't have a child, then they are working in prostitution. When I was in Hanawon, there was a nice girl who was pretty and I never imagined that she would be that kind of girl, because she was so good. But she wasn't married, didn't have kids, and she said she stayed with relatives. But later I found out that wasn't all. She lived like that (in prostitution).

This is the only method for poor and illegal North Korean women to live on the Chinese side of the borderland, and is different from the borderland experiences of men. The positions of North Korean women within this space are those of mother, wife, and daughter-in-law and, if this is not the case, the women fulfil the sexual desires of the men who possess economic power.

North Korean women are thus experiencing unilateral violence against the erased position of women within China and North Korean society. In the borderland constructed through the flow of diverse social relationships, North Korean women are the most marginalized minority and are exposed to dual suppression, between being illegal migrants and being the weak gender within power relationships. The borderland that is perceived and embodied by North Korean women is an unequal, confusing and unfair space where an exploitative structure functions.

Conclusion

Looking at the North Korean border-crossers from a multi-layered perspective is not an easy task, given that the Korean peninsula is the only divided nation in the world with a Cold War system acutely functioning in the post-Cold War period. Within the framework of the Cold War, encountering the extreme human rights situation of North Korean border-crossers is commonplace. Additionally, the fluctuating internal situation in North Korea, along with the horror of the detention center facilities experienced upon forced repatriation to the north, have become widely recognized symbols of the oppression of the North Korean regime.

This perspective is significant in the sense that it reveals the agony and hardship endured by the border crossers. But there is also a problem in simplifying the process of migration of the border crossers to South Korea and the drive towards locating a single variable, such as a political reason or the severe economic crisis. There is a limit to explaining various facts, including the fact that a large number of the North Korean border crossers, despite their illegal status, remain in China, that a majority of North Korean border crossers in the borderland are from North Hamgyong Province, and that a considerable number of North Korean border crossers repeatedly re-enter North Korea. In order to surmount these limitations, this article has sought to assert that the border crossing by the North Koreans is not migration based on a single reason, but instead stems from the construction of a space in their daily lives over a long period, a space known as the borderland. Many of the North Korean border-crossers who enter South Korea from Hamgyong Province sense the Sino-North Korea borderland as a single place rather than as a place divided by a national border. The Sino-North Korea borderland is a part of the North Koreans' intimate lifeworld and, as the economic crisis became aggravated, they engaged in border crossings without giving it much thought.

It is clear that the Sino-North Korea borderland is a region comprised of the territories of two modern nations adjacent to one another, centering on the Tumen and Amnok Rivers. If the politically formalized division of space functions as an "absolute space," there is also the existence of 'relative space" or "everyday space" in the daily lives of the people who have their roots there, and who live there. Thus, separate from the state level of space, the everyday space constructed through daily communication and exchanges by residents is not divided by a national border but is structured in an expanded form according to the people's line of mobility. This everyday space becomes a "place" through the various experiences and perceptions of actors, creating a sense of everydayness and intimacy. The closeness of the place, which is perceived through the familiar scenery, smells, sounds, relationships with people, and so forth, is the main cultural backdrop and resource behind the actions of the 300,000 to one million North Korean border-crossers crossing over to China's side of the borderland.

Of course the Sino-North Korea borderland is perceived differently by different actors: it is not simply a homogenized space in the globalized era but is experienced by actors through the politics of unequal and unbalanced space from within actual daily life. While the experienced Sino-North Korea borderland is a space of potential through the flow of daily communication and exchange, it is also, for some, a space of inequality, violence, and exploitation. It is a space for opportunity for North Korean women to overcome the economic crisis as well as a place where they can form a sense of closeness through everyday experiences and perceptions; but it is also a place of inequality where women are bound within the patriarchal system or are made to serve as sexual targets.

Furthermore, the borderland, which has expanded to include the South Koreans and South Korean economy, has not simply remained a geopolitical Sino-North Korea borderland but has continued to expand into other cities in China as well as crossings of the North and South Korea borders. This confirms that, amidst the long-running confrontational North and South Korea relationship, and despite North Korea being understood as a thoroughly isolated nation, it continues to change through the flow of exchanges and relationships through actors in the everyday dimension. This is one more way in which to make more complex our overly simplified understandings of North Korea.

Funding

This work is funded by the National Research Foundation of Korea [NRF-2014S1A3A2043571].

Notes

1. The Arduous March refers to the North Korean famine that occurred from 1995 to 1998. After the death of Kim Il-Sung, the economic situation of North Korea dramatically deteriorated. It is generally agreed that a minimum of one million deaths occurred between 1995 and 1998 due to the Arduous March.
2. Neoclassical economics of migration explains labor migration in the process of economic development. It basically theorizes international migration in relation to supply and demand of labor. Bringing in a more micro approach, neoclassical economics argues that a migrant is a rational actor who carefully calculates cost-benefit. As neoclassical economics have been criticized in many ways, the new economics of migration theory attempts to revise it and to bring in new insights that migration decisions are made by larger units of related people such as families rather than solely by individual actors (Massey et al. 1993, 431–440).
3. There are slight differences in the stated length of the border. According to Onishi in *The New York Times*, the length is 1,400 km long; another leading scholar in South Korea offers 1,376 km (O. Lee 2011).
4. Travel permission to China lasts for 90 days, but in recent years the permissible stay has been reduced to 60 days (*Radio Free Asia*, September, 25, 2014). To gain travel permission to China, bribery money of US$100–200 is typically needed.
5. There is no official data for this. However, during fieldwork in Dandong in Summer 2015, a North Korean government officer stated that there are 30,000 legal North Korean workers in Dandong, working in light industry and restaurants, mostly joint ventures between China and North Korea. North Korea offers labor and Chinese businessmen invest capital for raw materials and production sites.
6. Their salary is between 250–300 US dollars per month. Chinese businessmen normally pay workers' salaries to personnel from the state political security department. The North Korean government gives only 150–180 US dollars to the workers, and the rest goes to the government (KOTRA report 2014; interview with an ethnic Korean businessman who employs 200 North Korean workers in his factory).

References

Aldrich, R. 2011. "An Examination of China's Treatment of North Korean Asylum Seekers." *North Korean Review* 7 (1): 36–48.

Balibar, E. 1998. "The Borders of Europe." In *Cosmopolitics: Thinking and Feeling Beyond the Nation*, edited by P. Cheah and B. Robbins, Translated by J.Swenson, 216–233. London and Minneapolis: University of Minnesota Press.

Baud, M., and W. Schendel. 1997. "Towards a Comparative History of Borderlands." *Journal of World History* 8 (2): 211–242.

Brednikova, O., and V. Voronkov. 2000. "Border and Social Space Restructuring." www.indepsocres.spb.ru/bredvv_e.htm/.

Cho, Young Ju. 2011. "Inmin Mandeul Gi, Bukhanui Gender Jungchi [Making the People' and Gender Politics in North Korea: Distribution and Partisan System]." *Korea Women's Studies* 29 (2): 111–142.

Chu, Julie Y. 2010. *Cosmologies of Credit: Transnational Mobility and the Politics of Destination in China*. Durham, NC: Duke University Press.

Demick, Barbara. 2012. "China hires tens of thousands of North Korean guest workers." *Los Angeles Times*, 1 July. http://articles.latimes.com/2012/jul/01/world/la-fg-china-workers-20120701.

Gamburd, M. 2000. *The Kitchen Spoon's Handle: Transnationalism and Sri Lanka's Migrant Housemaids*. Ithaca, NY and London: Cornell University Press.

Inminnet, December 19th, 2013. http://korea.cpc.people.com.cn/65106/65130/69621/15376879.html.

Horstmann, H. 2002. "Incorporation and Resistance: Borderlands, Transnational Communities and Social Changes in South Asia." Unpublished Paper.

Kim, Sung Kyung. 2012. "Gyunghum deineun bukjeong gyeonggye jiyeok gwa edong [Experiencing North Korea-China Borderland and Routes of Mobility: 'Border-crossing' of North Korean border-crossers and the Expanding of Transnational Ethnic Spaces]." *Space and Society* 22 (2): 114–158.

Koo, Ji Young. 2011. "Segyehwa sidae ui hangukin ui iju wa chogukjeok sahwi gonggan [The Migration of Koreans in the Era of Globalization and Transnational Social Space – the Example of Qingdao, China]." *Korea Ethnic Culture* 40: 421–457.

Koo, Ji Young. 2013. "Dongbuk Asia eseoui iju wa jangso mandeulgi [Migration in North East Asia and Place-making – the example of Korean town in Qingdao, China]." *Northeast Culture Studies* 37: 269–289.

Korean Human Rights Commission. 2009. *Research on Human Rights Violation for North Korean Women*. Seoul: Korean Human Rights Commission.

KOTRA Beijing. 2014. *Jungguk nae bukhan nodongjaui hyunhwang* [Current Status of North Korean Workers in China]. Seoul: Korea.

Kwon, June Hee. 2015. "The Work of Waiting: Love and Money in Korean Chinese Transnational Migration." *Cultural Anthropology* 30 (3): 477–500.

Kwon, Tai-Hwan, and Kwang-Sung Park. 2004. "Joseonjeok ui ingu idong gwa younghyang [Population Movement of Korean Chinese and Its Impacts on Their Communities: A Case Study]." *Korea Population* 27 (2): 61–89.

Lee, Hwa Jin. 2011. "Talbuk yeoseong uk isung gwan gye ul tonghae bon inkwonchimhae gujo wad ae ung [The Structural Abuses of Human Rights and Coping Methods that Women Defectors from North Korea: Focusing on Relationships with the Opposite Sex in Emigrant Experience]." *Peace Studies*. Autumn: 367–404.

Lee, Ok-hee. 2011. *Bukjung jeopgyeong jiyeok: jeon hwan gi bukjung jeopgyeong jiyeok uk dosi network* [North Korea and China Borderland: City Network in the Borderland]. Seoul: Purungil.

Lee, Young Hyung. 2012. *Russia uk geukdong baljeon gwa bukhan nodongja* [Russia's Far East Development and North Korean Workers]. Korea Institute of National Unification(KINU) Research Series 12–03. Seoul: KINU.

Lee, Hye-Kyung, Kiseon Chung, Myungki Yoo, and Minjung Kim. 2006. "Ijunui yeosunghwa wa chogukjeok gajeok: joseongjeok saraeul jeongsimuro [Feminization of Migration and Transnational Families of Korean-Chinese Migrants in South Korea]." *Korea Sociology* 40 (5): 258–298.

Massey, D. 1999. "Power-Geometries and the Politics of Space-Time." In *Hettner Lecture 1998*. Heidelberg: University of Heidelberg. https://publishup.uni-potsdam.de/opus4-ubp/.../gr2_00_ERez09.pdf.

Massey, Douglas S., Joaquin Arango, Graeme Hugo, Ali Kouaouci, Adela Pellegrino, and J. Taylor. 1993. "Theories of International Migration: A Review and Appraisal." *Population and Development Review* 19 (3): 431–466.

Ministry of Foreign Affair. 2014. "Jaewei dongpo hyunhwang [Current Status of Overseas Koreans]." Accessed September 5, 2015. http://www.mofa.go.kr/travel/overseascitizen/

Ministry of Unification. 2016. "Bukhanitaljumin uk hyunhwang [Current Status of North Korean Arrivals]." Accessed June 22, 2016. www.unikorea.org.kr

Newman, D., and A. Paasi. 1998. "Fences and neighbours in the postmodern world: boundary narratives in political geography." *Progress in Human Geography* 22 (2): 186–207.
Pinilla, Daniel Goma. 2004. "Border Disputes between China and North Korea." *China Perspectives*, 52 March-April: 1–8.
Radio Free Asia, September 25th, 2014. http://www.rfa.org/english/news/korea.
Ravenstein, Ernest Georg. 1889. "The Laws of Migration." *Journal of the Royal Statistical Society* 52 (2): 241–305.
Sassen, S. 1991. *The Global City: New York, London, Tokyo*. Princeton NJ: Princeton University Press.
Seo, Jae Jin. 2005. "Bukhan ui seongbun chabyul jeongcheki sijangyoso hwaksane michin younghyang [Impact of Social Class Discrimination Policy on the Development of Market Elements in North Korea]." *Korean Unification Research* 44: 89–109.
Smith, Hazel. 2012. Explaining North Korean Migration to China. Woodrow Wilson Centre: NKIDP e-Dossier.
Takamura, K. 2004. "Not 'Divided Places', But 'A Living Space': Chinese Women on the Thai-Malaysian Border." *Journal of Asian and African Studies* 68: 173–191.
Vaughan-Williams, N. 2009. *Border Politics: The Limits of Sovereign Power*. Edinburgh: Edinburgh University Press.
Wendle, T., and M. Rosler, 1999. "Frontiers and Borderlands: The Rise and Relevance of an Anthropological Perspectives" In *Frontiers and Borderlands: Anthropological Perspectives*, edited by Michael Rosler and Tobias Wendl, 1–30. Munich: University of Munich.
Yanhap News. July 30th, 2014. http://www.yonhapnews.co.kr/.

The Thai-Burmese borderland: mobilities, regimes, actors and changing political contexts

Petra Dannecker and Wolfram Schaffar

For decades people from Myanmar have fled or migrated to Thailand. Civil conflicts, political repression, poverty and a lack of work opportunities are just some of the reasons why people have left Myanmar. Through these movements and the way they have been governed, a borderland has been constituted. In recent decades especially, the border itself has been strategically manipulated by state authorities to preserve a border area used as an industrial node for export-oriented industries dependent on cheap (i.e. migrant) labor. This article discusses the processes establishing the systemic categories of "refugee" and "labor migrant." On the basis of fieldwork conducted from 2012 on, the article also analyzes the influence on the borderland of recent political and economic changes in Thailand and Myanmar.

Introduction

For decades people from Myanmar have fled or migrated to Thailand. Civil conflicts, political repression, poverty and a lack of work opportunities are just some of the reasons why people have left Myanmar. Although it is difficult to estimate how many people have crossed the border to Thailand, it is said that in 2011 alone 1.5 million Burmese were resident in Thailand (Eberle and Holliday 2011, 371). Through these movements and the way they were and are governed, a borderland has been constituted, which can be characterized through specific forms of exchange, selective integration and forms of control. The meaning and function of the Thai-Burmese border, as a geopolitical demarcation, have changed accordingly. Soe Lin Aung (2014, 27) argues that, in recent decades especially, the "border line itself" has been strategically manipulated by state authorities to preserve a border area for use as an industrial node for export-oriented industries and, as such, has led to an industrialization process dependent on cheap (i.e. migrant) labor. The borderland, however, is also increasingly constituted and structured by the movements of the undocumented and organized "around a minimizing [of] contact with state authorities" (Soe Lin Aung 2014, 28).

Given this context, the main aim of this paper is twofold. In the first part we analyze how the different groups of people who have crossed the border were and are categorized and governed according to the specific interests of transnational capital and the state authorities, as well as by, for example, humanitarian organizations; and what implications this had and has for them. We will briefly describe and historicize the construction process of the categories and show how, as part of this process, refugee and migrant worker systems have been established to govern the borderland. Assuming, however, that categories and borders are constructed and therefore permanently negotiated, and that migrants and refugees (along with other actors) are part of "doing borders" (Hess and Tsianos 2007, 248) and drawing boundaries through their own regulations and practice, the negotiations and the conflicts between the various local, national and transnational actors will be scrutinized. Theoretically and methodologically this view draws on anthropological approaches to the investigation of borders and borderlands, as outlined in Chan (2013), Horstmann (2011a, 2011b), Cunningham and Heyman (2004) and Gupta and Ferguson (1992). It also relies on literature on transnationalism such as the work of Ong (1999) and Mintz (1998).

Consequently the second part of the paper is based on fieldwork in the border area.[1] On the basis of this data[2] we analyze two fundamental shifts in the political and economic development of the region that have influenced the situation in this borderland between Thailand and Myanmar in general, and for the Burmese population in particular. We discuss the "opening" of Myanmar, which had been relatively isolated under the military dictatorship between 1962 and 2010, and touch upon the changes occurring on the Thai side in the wake of the recent military *coup d'état*, which brought to power a regime with specific ambitions to handle "security issues" including the question of Burmese citizens in Thailand. How these political and economic processes affect the borderland and its categories, communities and agencies is therefore our focus. The main aim of the paper is to scrutinize these political and economic transformations not from the often state-centered perspective on borders, but from a borderland perspective. This will allow us to show that although the categorization of the Burmese in the borderland follows a set of particular ideologies closely connected to security issues and global economic restructuring, it is simultaneously a constantly changing social space of struggle and contestation.

Categorizing migrants versus refugees: a historical account of the landscape of power in the borderland

Long before the drawing-up of the border during Thailand's and Myanmar's nation-building processes, people from Burma[3] fled or migrated and were welcomed into Siam (Lee 2007, 24): "Siamese kings made use of the immigrants as useful laborers and border guards" (Wyatt 2004, 113). This points to a long history of social, cultural and economic exchanges constituting the borderland between Siam/Thailand and Burma/Myanmar. Mobility was part of the daily life of the people in that region even before being confronted with the so-called modernizing influences of European expansion from the sixteenth century onward. The categorization of the people crossing the border between the two countries and their movements has its roots in colonial history; the demarcation of the Burma–Siam border as well as the division of Burma into several regions took place under British rule (Pongsawat 2007, Thongchai Winichakul 1994), whereas the lowland areas with a mainly Burman population – so-called Central Burma – was integrated into the Indian colonial administration. The people in the hilly regions surrounding this area were not under direct rule and could maintain a socio-political structure and agency primarily oriented against central authorities (Scott 2010).

After independence in 1947, British ethnic categorization was maintained and the country was divided into several ethnically determined administrative units. Areas of Central Burma with a predominantly Burmese population were split into seven divisions (since the constitution of 2008, the "divisions" have been re-named as "regions"). The areas at the country's periphery became seven states (Shan-, Rakhine-, Kachin-,

Chin-, Kayah-, Karen-, and Mon-State), named after the ethnic groups said to form the majority living in each. The distribution of the ethnic population, however, does not always match the constructed borders of the states. Many Karen, for example, live in other states, which is true of many other ethnic groups as well. This administrative structure, in particular negotiations concerning a constitutional framework for the newly founded union, led from the outset to conflicts and widespread violence within the country. The Karen National Union (KNU) and, later in the 1960s, other ethnic insurgent groups like the Shan State Army or the Kachin Independence Army were founded as a result of this conflict and tried to resist the nation-building process that had been implemented by the army as the central institution of the state (Callahan 2003; South 2008). From the 1960s onward especially, political leaders from ethnic groups were sidelined or eliminated and replaced by members of the ruling Burmese Socialist Program Party, intensifying the already strained relationship between the center and the periphery (Smith 1999; cf. Maung Thawnghmung 2012). Military incursions into ethnic territories in the border regions since have not only meant hardship for the population but destroyed the regions' economic foundations. Nevertheless, economic activities between Thailand and Burma, which throughout their history have structured the borderland, continued especially with regard to trade.

Despite incursions by the Burmese military, the border areas in Burma fell partly under the control of different ethnic organizations or parties; for instance, the eastern border area was under the KNU. Thailand tried to integrate its remote border areas, so-called "wasteland," into the national economy from the 1980s onward, with injections of national and transnational capital. This policy, which aimed to "develop" the so-called less developed Thai border regions, led to internal migration as well as labor migration from Burma. The Thai government, interested in filling the factories with cheap migrant workers, did not restrict immigration, thereby revealing the "intersection of global and situated elements" (Ong 2007, 5). Through industrialization processes initiated by government policies as well as the Asian Development Bank, Mae Sot, for example, a town close to the border with Burma in the north-west of Thailand, not only developed into a central node for regional economic integration (Soe Lin Aung 2014, 30) but also became an important place for Burmese migrants seeking work in expanding industries. Simultaneously, domestic migrants from other parts of Thailand settled in the border regions, engaging in business not only but primarily with Burmese traders who regularly crossed back and forth into Thailand. Customer gates along the border were established and black markets flourished throughout the borderland. Not only traders and goods but also members of ethnic minorities used these gates and trading routes to cross the border to Thailand due to conflict in their regions, especially from the 1960s onwards. By the 1980s, the borderland had been constituted and can be characterized by intensive interaction between Thai locals and people from Burma involved in trade and business. While many Burmese crossed the border regularly as traders, others settled and worked in one of the new factories, in agriculture, or in construction around the border space (Lee 2011). Until the 1980s no official distinction between "illegal" and "legal" or "formal" and "informal" migrants or refugees was made. Due to the specific context and the interests of the different actors involved, such categories were meaningless (Lee 2007, 61). It was only in the 1980s that both the pattern of border crossing as well as the political framework in which it occurred changed significantly.

Interestingly, the literature analyzing migration between Burma and Thailand up to the late 1980s does not distinguish between migrants and refugees, and the ethnic background of those crossing the border is hardly ever emphasized. Taking into account that the border between Burma and Thailand is approximately 2400 km long, crossing it was part of everyday life for at least the people of the borderland (see also Scott 2010). As mentioned above, political actors such as the Thai government accepted this situation for economic and political reasons, whereas the Burmese military regime was never able to gain control over the border region. The fact that ethnic groups in Burma "controlled" the borders as well as the trade routes was thus accepted or ignored by the Thai authorities, at least as long as the Burmese government was seen as a "communist" threat and formalized economic relationships did not exist. So the migration of, for example, Karen crossing the border to Thailand or Shan crossing primarily the northern border was for many years not a prominent political or security issue.

Political changes in the late 1980s in both Burma and Thailand had a tremendous influence on the borderland with regard to migration and to the categorization of people crossing the border. Different actors played important roles. In the 1980s Burma witnessed severe economic problems as well as anti-government protests. Starting in the cities and the universities in 1988 the protests spread to the whole country and involved people from different sectors. The demonstrations were harshly suppressed and after a military coup a new administrative structure, the State and Law Council, was installed. Not only were Burmese dissidents forced to flee to neighboring countries – mainly Thailand – but thousands also left in search of better opportunities abroad. Others fled conflict zones in the ethnic regions after traumatic experiences, poverty, or forced labor (ND-Burma 2010, 7 in Soe Lin Aung 2014). Through the new administrative structure in Burma, government officials were sent all over the country to fulfill military as well as administrative tasks such as, for example, border control or the implementation of so-called development projects. Whereas in Kachin state a ceasefire agreement was signed improving the living situation of the population (Callahan 2007; Zaw Oo and Win Min 2007, 51), the equivalent was never achieved in Karen state. Warfare continued with the Karen National Union (KNU) and led to the devastation of a large part of Karen state, especially in the border region (Smith 1999). Not surprisingly, Karen were therefore increasingly pushed across the border to Thailand after 1988, while others who stayed inside Myanmar became internally displaced (Lee 2007, 64).

As for Thailand, the ending of the Indochinese conflicts led to a reorientation in Thai politics, and new political and economic strategies were developed that explicitly concerned relations with neighboring countries. In this context a formalization of economic ties with neighboring countries, including Burma, was desired. Several projects were negotiated with the military government in Burma, especially involving logging concessions. This led to a further deterioration of the economy in Karen state because the black market declined and the military began to encroach close to the border, increasingly attacking the local civilian support bases of the KNU in order to secure its grip on natural resources. This situation led to a new influx of Burmese into Thailand. In contrast to previous inward migrations, the size of the flows increased tremendously and was so enormous that in some towns, like Mae Sot, the Burmese outnumbered the Thai locals (Lee 2007, 66).

Burmese settlements – mainly Karen – had already existed in the Thai border regions before this new influx of migrants, but were previously more "village-like." The newer camps or settlements were comparatively open, providing a relatively safe and secure space beyond the Thai-Burmese border. The management of these settlements was primarily in the hands of the migrants themselves, while the Thai national and local governments were in charge of security. Only a few local and international NGOs were involved, mainly in providing basic goods. Thompson (2008) argues that until the late

1980s the administration of these camps resembled very closely systems their residents had "brought with them."

Many Burmese migrants worked in Thai or multinational factories, often built in cooperation with overseas partners from Hong Kong and Taiwan. The factories were strategically set up near the border due the availability of cheap Burmese labor. The relocation of factories from parts of central Thailand to the border area was an aspect of the Thai government's decentralization policy in the context of the economic boom of the late 1980s and early 1990s. Migrant laborers were largely hired "undocumented" at least until the late 1990s, when the Thai government introduced a first registration scheme. Until the mid-1990s however, there had been no institutional, legal, temporary employment channel for unskilled workers (Kaur 2010, 16), nor was a systemic distinction made between so-called labor migrants and refugees. Those living in the camp-like settlements were engaged as factory workers or in various other economic activities and none of the actors involved was keen to categorize the Burmese migrants, who had become a significant and important feature of the Thai economy and society in the borderland (Myat Mon 2010, 36).

Thailand is one of the countries that has never signed the Geneva Convention on the status of refugees or the 1967 Protocol, and Thai national law does not provide any basis for handling refugees. The Thai government therefore never formally recognized Burmese migrants as refugees although, starting from 1997 onward, Thai authorities allowed the UNHCR to operate in Thailand, mainly because they were no longer able to handle the migration situation due to the new influx. It became increasingly obvious that the already existing camps were difficult to maintain not only because of continuous growth but due also to the fact that security was growing increasingly problematic. Members of insurgent groups recruited migrants from the camps and began to get involved in camp management, which led to conflicts between different actors (Horstmann 2012). Given this situation, the Thai government decided to enhance its control by implementing a policy of reducing the number of camps from thirty in 1994 to nine in 1998 (Bowles 1998). It has been argued that the Thai government intended to make the border area safer and less vulnerable to attacks by the different parties to the conflict. Whose security was in focus, however, must be questioned, since the human rights of the migrants were grossly violated. Fences were erected around the former settlements, mobility was restricted, and working outside the camps was no longer officially permitted. The Thai military took control of the camps and only limited autonomous administration was permitted. Consequently, the livelihoods of those in the camps were eradicated and the residents became entirely dependent on outside aid (Walter 2012, 44). This was the moment when humanitarian relief agencies began to get involved in higher numbers and became important actors in the borderland, especially in the camps. During the implementation of this policy of "securitization," the Burmese living in the camps were increasingly characterized as refugees – and ultimately were made refugees.

The situation of Burmese migrants who lived close to and worked in the factories also changed. Although garment and textile factories in the border region (especially in Mae Sot) had become dependent on Burmese migrant labor (Kaur 2010; Thornton 2006), the Thai government in 1992 started to use the Foreign Employment Act of 1978 to manage migration through annual registration. This registration scheme was, however, "primarily concerned with controlling migrants, knowing their whereabouts and allowing for the deportation of any migrant who [was] not registered" (Kaur 2010, 16). Additionally, annual registration was a financial burden for migrants and, due to regular deportations, the system effectively increased human trafficking back into

Thailand (Pollock 2005). With the implementation of the registration system, anyone who did not live inside the camps and who did not register was categorized as undocumented. These unregistered migrants, who always outnumbered registered workers, were increasingly subject to raids and prosecution.[4]

The situation did not improve when in 2003 Thailand and Myanmar signed a Memorandum of Understanding on employment cooperation, allowing the recruitment and employment of less-skilled workers from Myanmar for a period of two years. This was the first time that the Myanmar junta acknowledged that millions of migrants were looking for work in Thailand (Myat Mon 2010, 36). Registration depended, however, on the cooperation of employers, who deducted the costs from the workers' salaries. Moreover, these early registration cards did not grant mobility within Thailand. Thus the system effectively increased the laborer's dependence on her/his employer, a strategy well known within Asia and beyond (Kaur 2010 or Dannecker 2012). In 2009, yet another registration scheme, called "nationality verification," was introduced. This scheme was intended for workers who were already residing in Thailand. Since for this process, identity cards or passports were needed, it allowed not only the Thai government but also the Myanmar government to demonstrate their authority and power in the border region. In the early stage of implementation, the Burmese government made the process very complicated and bureaucratic and for quite some time did not take any concrete steps to verify the citizenship of Burmese migrants (Kaur 2010). This was experienced especially by members of ethnic minorities, with the exception of the Rohingya Muslims, that are formally citizens of the state but not perceived or treated as equal citizens by the ethnic Burmese in power (Holliday 2014, 412).

Thus, in the course of the last two decades, mobility combined with political, social and economic transformations has caused a dramatic change in the borderland, not exclusively yet especially with regard to the categorization of Burmese immigrants. High mobility is not a new phenomenon in this area but, as Scott (2010) impressively shows, the formal and legal categorization of the mobile population is a recent phenomenon that has led to a migration regime subdivided into refugee and migrant laborer regimes.[5] The regime approach is chosen here because it allows for an integrated analysis of the historical processes at play, the discourses and debates put forward by different actors, and the empirical, quantitative data. Regimes are characterized by dynamic interactions and by the regulation of social relations (see for example Karakayali and Tsianos 2007, 14 with regard to migration regimes). Moreover, regimes are conceptualized as a product of negotiations between different actors. This allows for an analysis of the complex processes and transformations observed in the borderland. The borderland migration regime can at present be divided into refugee and labor migration regimes intended to control mobility and to clarify inclusion and exclusion while being at the same time contested. Both exist and are presented, at least formally, as independent from each other. The refugee regime came into being from the mid-1990s onward as more and more people left Burma, the control of the nation-states increased and international humanitarian organizations entered the arena. The labor migrant regime is a result of new policies introduced in 2003 and the Memorandum of Understanding between Thailand and Burma. Despite the official picture of them as discrete entities, both the labor migration and refugee regimes are closely interrelated and structure the current situation in the borderland. At first glance, the Thai national government seemed to be the decisive actor that, as a manifestation of state power, developed policies and strategies to control and categorize the flow of people who, by virtue of their mobility, permanently challenge the authority and influence of the state.

However, many more actors are actively involved in these processes; this can and should not be ignored. First of all, the migrants and refugees who challenge and transgress the categories imposed on them; second, entrepreneurs who depend on migrant labor and who negotiate their interests vis-à-vis the political interests of the government on different levels; and last, international humanitarian organizations working in the camps to improve refugees' situation and legal status.

This brief discussion of the borderland shows that the concept of a nation tied to a bounded geographic space and separating citizens from non-citizens implies not just the control of territory but also the control of mobilities. As the historical overview has shown, post-modern subjects can no longer avoid the influence of the nation-state, even in the borderlands or peripheries (Lee 2011, 81). The two regimes that have developed in the Thai-Myanmar borderland are a result of contested state-building and modernization processes involving different actors with conflicting interests and strategies, and reveal that borders are not fixed over time and space. These actors and their rationalities as well as the implications of recent political changes in Myanmar and in Thailand will be explored in the following sections.

Two regimes of mobility: two sets of fundamental problems

The tendencies outlined above can clearly be seen in Mae Sot, a border town on the river Moei that has emerged as a hub for Thai-Myanmar cross-border relations and an important transit point (Lee 2011, 82). Within a relatively small area we find refugee camps of mainly Karen refugees, industrial production sites relying on migrant workers, clinics serving mobile people from the entire region, NGOs and advocacy organizations working for migrants and refugees, restaurants and tea shops serving various ethnic groups and acting as a public space in which to meet and debate, and border police and various Thai state institutions dealing with border issues. The density of institutions and actors working on or in relation to cross-border relations has made Mae Sot an ideal site for empirical social research. As in other border towns too, the social, economic, political and administrative developments in Mae Sot led to a situation where people moving across the Moei River to Mae Sot were categorized as one of two groups – either migrant workers or refugees. As argued by Hess and Tsianos (2007), this categorization is a social process in which categories and categorizations are constantly negotiated and reproduced by the different actors involved. Authorities in Mae Sot and in Myawaddy (the town on the Myanmar side), the migrants themselves, and many academics have conceptualized these two groups as strictly distinct from each other, and both categories are presented as entailing their own specific problems. However, as this discussion has shown, the categories developed to control the borderland are the result of political as well as social conflicts and are therefore contested.

Migrant workers

As far as the group of migrant workers is concerned, their problems are mainly connected with their legal status and, for many, their lack of documents. A little ferry beneath the Thai-Myanmar Friendship Bridge in Mae Sot makes it possible for people from the Myanmar side of the Moei River to enter Thailand without any problems, whether they have documents or not. There seem to be no emigration or immigration procedures on either side of the river, and the authorities appear to tolerate this kind of movement as part of informal small-scale border traffic (field observation, April 2012).

Apart from the ferry below the Friendship Bridge, there seem to be more informal ways of entering Thai territory elsewhere along the river (expert interviews, April 2012).

Officially speaking, however, people who have entered through these channels lack proper documents and are considered "illegal" immigrants. The way the border police present the problems entailed by this illegal status and the question of who is affected by it and who is to be blamed for it is somewhat inconsistent. On the one hand, it is the illegal status *as such* and those individuals bearing it who are perceived to be a problem. "Illegal" immigrants are seen as having breached Thai law and might thus be a source of all kinds of trouble, such as petty crime (exchange with the border police in Mae Sot, April 2012). On the other hand, and in contrast to the first perspective, undocumented immigration is seen as problematic not due to the immigrants per se but to human traffickers, a perception that increasingly dominates migration management and migration discourses worldwide. From this perspective, immigrants are not seen primarily as having breached the law but as victims of other perpetrators.

Migrants themselves see their lack of documents as the major source of their problems. First, they complain of being exposed to arbitrary police actions on the grounds of their status. It is reported that migrants being chased through the streets by the police is a common scene in Mae Sot (interview with experts/NGOs in Mae Sot). The intimidation caused by public persecution such as this leads to severe restriction on mobility and limits migrants' room for maneuver in public spaces (Arnold 2013; Pearson and Kusakabe 2012; Zaw Aung 2010). This can be defined as an important strategy of control and governance in the borderland. Second, the lack of documents exposes migrants to exploitation by factory owners, who take advantage of their vulnerable status and refuse to pay the Thai minimum wage, or deduct considerable sums as fees for accommodation, security, or other alleged expenditures (Arnold 2013; Pearson and Kusakabe 2012). Likewise, traffickers exploit the situation of vulnerability and – in collaboration with the employer – draw commission fees directly from workers' salaries (Kaur 2010; Integrated Regional Information Networks [IRIN] 2013; Schearf 2013; Zaw Aung 2010). In sum, the lack of documents and the resulting illegal status is seen as a major source of vulnerability that is exploited by traffickers/brokers, the police, and employers – sometimes in cooperation between all three, revealing the politically, economically and socially shaped landscape of power (Soe Lin Aung 2014).

In this context it is, however, important to note that migrants, despite the actions of Thai authorities, also structure the borderland space. Their initial mobility itself, but also their cross-border circulation to "…mitigate against threats to their safety and stability" (Soe Lin Aung 2014, 33), as well as a number of self-protection strategies or forms of resistance like drawing on community networks or organizing regular strikes or protests, demonstrate the migrants' agency (see Soe Lin Aung 2014, 35). Added to this is their onward migration, whenever possible, to Bangkok – described by Lee (2011) as the "Bangkok dream." It is necessary to understand these activities, as well as those of the authorities, to comprehend the social, political and economic dynamics of the borderland.

Refugees

The issue of refugees has been discussed in a very different way. For a long time, the international community's system of organizing their whereabouts in Thailand and their movement to third countries was considered the central problem. According to international standards, there are three possible solutions to dealing with large numbers of refugees, such as there have been in Thailand. The most desirable is timely repatriation to the place of origin after the reasons for fleeing have been resolved. Local integration is considered the second best option, since it allows refugees to stay relatively close to their place of origin and spares them further displacement. Resettlement in a third country is seen as the least desirable option. Of these options, Myanmar refugees in Thailand were left for many years with the least desirable option.[6]

Repatriation was ruled out for the past two decades, since the armed conflict between the Karen insurgent groups and the central government – the very reason for refugees to flee the country – continued with varying intensity (South 2011). The Thai authorities, not wanting to give up control of selective integration according to their needs, have not been willing to accept local integration. Moreover, as mentioned already, Thailand has not signed the Geneva Convention and will not do so, which is why Thailand does not adhere to UNHCR principles and cannot be forced on legal grounds to do so (Walter 2012). Although resettlement to a third country was therefore the policy of choice, there was a consistent mismatch between the high numbers of refugees needing a place on the official resettlement program and the main recipient countries' relatively low refugee quotas. Despite this mismatch, the quota of the biggest recipient county, the US, could not in recent years be filled with people willing to resettle (Walter 2012). The reasons are complex and show that the resettlement decision is not taken, on the part of the refugees, on an abstract basis. Rather, social affiliations inside the camp or to the place of origin in Myanmar play a crucial role (Walter 2012).

All actors involved construed life in the camps as transitory. The administration of the camp, the education of children, and the economic basis of everyday life: everything was and is organized as if for a short transitional phase. For a certain group, especially young refugees who have opted for resettlement, this was definitely the case (Lee 2011). Others, however, who have spent large parts of their lives or have even been born in the camps – which have already existed for two decades – call them home (interviews in Mae La camp, as well as with experts in Mae Sot, April 2012).

Blurring boundaries

The Thai state authorities have invested quite a lot in the infrastructure backing up the two regimes of mobility. In addition to fencing in the refugee camps, checkpoints have been set up at the entrances and along the streets leading to the camps. There is also a checkpoint, an immigration office and a police station directly at the aforementioned Friendship Bridge, so that everyone passing by is either registered or arrested. All these checkpoints and police offices are well staffed. At times, raids are a common picture in downtown Mae Sot, with illegal immigrants being chased and picked up by the police. But despite the physical presence of the state apparatus, the entire regulatory regime has always been quite porous. Mobile people, no matter whether they were officially categorized as refugees or migrants, have developed coping strategies that demonstrate a high level of creativity and agency.

Some of the strategies observed are quite open. Underneath the Friendship Bridge with its fenced immigration booths and police checkpoints, there is a little boat that commutes between the river banks and transports people from one side to the other without any immigration procedure. The fact that this informal migration flow happens directly under the eyes of the immigration police highlights their weak administrative capacity as well as habitually abusive governance, or underscores the contested and negotiated character of the entire regime. The same permeability was reported from the police checkpoints at the entrance of the refugee camps. In many camps, refugees were able to negotiate ways to leave the camp to engage in daily wage labor in the surrounding agricultural or industrial production sites. Arrangements included checkpoint "fees" or permission to bring food or consumer products into the camp for trade. These are cases in which the two categories established through legal and discursive frameworks – refugee vs. migrant worker – are indistinguishable. Refugees who in the course of their prolonged stays started leaving the camp for daily work can be seen as refugees-turned-workers. But switching identity also worked in the other direction. Since good-quality education was provided inside the camps through NGOs and international aid organizations, mobile parents often sent their children–there for their schooling, during which period they were categorized as refugees. In such cases it could happen that over a certain period of time members of the same family officially fell into different categories. Or, put differently, mobile people exercised their agency by changing and mixing their identities according to their actual needs – a strategy that can also be interpreted as an act of resistance against the border regime.

Reforms in Myanmar

Since the elections of 2010 and since President Thein Sein has taken office, Myanmar has embarked on a dynamic process of political change and opening-up that has surprised all analysts as well as those involved in the process in Myanmar itself. Although the military was, at least until the new government took power in April 2016, the most dominant force in the country and fully in control of decision-making processes, it seems that the reforms and the speed at which they unfolded have led to a momentum that cannot be stopped easily, as the elections and victory of the National League for Democracy (NLD) have proven (Cheesman, Skidmore, and Wilson 2010, 2012; Effner 2013).

The reforms have wrought fundamental changes to Myanmar's standing, both at the wider international level as well as in its bilateral relations with Thailand. The latter has also impacted the borderland and the way it is governed. In 2003 and 2009, bilateral agreements had already made it possible to address the problem of documentation at the local authority level on both sides of the border, through cooperation in the implementation of a system of so-called "nationality verification" for Burmese migrants. In line with its new openness however, the government of Myanmar has changed its perspective on its citizens abroad and has actively taken up the issue of abuse and migrant trafficking from Myanmar into Thailand (Integrated Regional Information Networks [IRIN] 2013). In a new round of active bilateral cooperation, it was the Myanmar authorities who pushed for a quicker and smoother procedure of nationality verification. Deadlines by which migrant workers must register or risk the real possibility of being deported had been tight, but the fact that they were extended several times demonstrates the willingness of the Myanmar authorities to bring about a change in the legal status of their citizens abroad (Schearf 2013). Instead of a long-awaited reprieve from the problems caused by their lack of legal status, however, migrant workers in the borderland did not see their situation improve as they might have expected (Pollock 2013). Throughout 2012 and 2013, new problems arose which at first seemed purely technical. Although it was pushed for by the Myanmar government in an attempt to take care of their citizens abroad, the process of nationality verification ran into problems. Deadlines were repeatedly extended but, until late 2013, the majority of migrant workers remained undocumented. Seemingly, the process was jeopardized by conflicting interests.

Even more telling is the breakdown of registration figures. Although Tak province, where Mae Sot is situated, is the hub for Myanmar migrant workers, the number of those newly registered in 2012–2013 was much lower than in any other part of Thailand. This was true of both the registration process based on the Memorandum of Understanding and the nationality verification process (Migrants Assistance Programme Foundation 2013). It was not only the length and complexity of the procedure or the high cost of $400 per person (a sum attributed to multi-layered corruption in the Thai system [Integrated Regional Information Networks (IRIN) 2013; Schearf 2013]) but specific obstacles within Tak province that prevented workers from getting documents. One reason, as Soe Lin Aung (2014) (drawing on Scott [2010]) argues, could be that migrants perceived the borderland as a space of refuge and self-protection, closely related to what Scott describes as the desire not to be governed by state authorities. In the most recent meetings between President Thein Sein of Myanmar and current Thai Prime Minister Prayuth in November 2014, the issue of national verification was taken up again, as will be addressed below.

A second problem that occurred during 2012–2013 adds to this picture. One of the biggest restrictions resulting from a lack of documents is the restriction of mobility. Migrant workers had to hide in public, and their immobility exposed them to exploitation by employers. Reports from late 2012, however, exposed that even migrants with documents were stopped at police checkpoints and were not allowed to move outside Mae Sot (Lawi Weng 2012).

That migrants are prevented in a systematic way from entering the process of nationality verification in Tak province and that, even if they have them, their documents do not suffice or are disregarded, reveals the constructed and contested nature of the discourse on migrant workers and their alleged problems. It exposes the conflicting interests underlying the construction of "illegal" migrants.

As outlined above, most of the production sites at the Mae Sot border area have been established quite recently and their entire business model relies on the availability of exceptionally cheap labor. With better living and working conditions in Central Thailand, and especially with the introduction of a minimum wage under the Thaksin government, this business model has been increasingly challenged. More and more, workers chose Mae Sot only as a transit point en route to Central Thailand (Lee 2011). Since mobility is an important indication of migrant agency, nationality verification that allows workers to move freely and enhances their bargaining power in claiming the minimum wage turned out to be a further blow to Mae Sot as a site of production.

This is why, through formal and informal cooperation between the Thai authorities and factory owners, the area of Mae Sot is organized as a "site of exception" (Ong 2006; Tan 2012). The police turned a blind eye to informal entry points and thus kept the border porous to make Mae Sot exceptionally accessible for people from Myanmar. The authorities, however, also protected informal structures and practices that allowed employers, as an exception to Thai law, to ignore the statutory minimum wage. The construction of the "illegality" of migrants was one of several means of institutionalizing evasion of the minimum wage and insulating the Mae Sot labor market and the borderland from the rest of Thailand. The average minimum wage for workers in Mae Sot seems to be around 60 baht per day, which is far below the legally guaranteed national minimum wage of 300 baht per day (Migrants Assistance Programme Foundation 2013; Pollock 2013). When new rounds of nationality verification granted a legal status to the migrants and threatened to undermine the basis of the business model, new obstacles were introduced in Tak province, such as informal checkpoints on the roads to central

Thailand, set up to make it exceptionally difficult to leave Mae Sot. Thus the governance as well as labor migrant regime in the borderland is dominated by state as well as economic authorities and interests. Nonetheless, migrants' cross-border and internal movements are resituating the political practice of space in the borderland as well (Soe Lin Aung 2014, 39).

The economic changes in Myanmar are even more dramatic than the administrative or political ones. Until recently, Myanmar played neither politically nor economically an important role for the West. Even for its biggest economic partner, China, Myanmar was not a high priority (Li 2012; Sutter 2012). From 2011 on, this has changed dramatically and Myanmar has succeeded in getting priority attention as a cooperation partner in the West as well as in China (Li 2012; Sun 2012). This change of perception can be seen in international engagement in Special Economic Zones (SEZ). Ambitious projects have been launched in Dawei, Kyaukpyu and Thilawa, where deep-sea ports and direct land connections to Thailand and China are being built (Naruemon Thabchumpon, Middleton, and Zaw Aung 2012, Slodkowski 2012). Since wages are still much lower than in neighboring countries like Thailand and Malaysia, dynamic economic growth is expected to be unleashed through SEZs, some of which offer work opportunities directly competing with productions sites on the other side of the border in Thailand, i.e. in the borderland.

Interestingly, parallel to informal strategies to maintain Mae Sot as a "site of exception," actors like the local authorities and factory owners are pushing for the establishment of an SEZ in Mae Sot (*Bangkok Post*, January 21, 2013; *The Nation*, June 3, 2012; Maung Shwe 2011). Usually, SEZs try to attract investors by granting tax exemptions or subsidizing energy or other costs. Local employers in Mae Sot, however, made it very clear that inside the SEZ the national minimum wage would not be paid (interviews, April 2012). This strategy can be seen as an attempt to formalize the "site of exception," very much in the sense of how Ong (2006) uses the term. The whole process is supported by the highest political levels (*Bangkok Post*, June 13, 2013) and aims to re-scale the entire migration and labor regime, not only in Mae Sot but on a regional cross-border level. What is being planned is a network of interrelated SEZ's that connects production sites in Myanmar and in Thailand (interview with the Mae Sot Chamber of Commerce, 2012; *Bangkok Post*, June 13, 2013; *Bangkok Post*, October 9, 2014).

Paradoxically, the formal establishment of SEZ's (i.e. sites of exception where national legislation such as the minimum wage does not apply) can be interpreted as a consolidation of state authority. As argued in Meehan (2011), Woods (2011), Tan (2012) and Schaffar (2008), the deliberate self-restraint of the regulatory sovereignty of the state can be regarded as a strategy of state-building and affirmation of state power. Thus, the SEZ policy is in line with earlier Thai and Myanmar state policies to consolidate their authority by "doing borders" and shaping new landscapes of power.

As for the problems of the second group, the refugees, the change was even more dramatic. The Karen National Union (KNU), which had fought the central government for decades in what qualified as the longest civil war in modern history, finally reached a ceasefire agreement with the government (*BBC News Asia*, January 12, 2012; Saw Thein Myint 2013). The peace process is currently being discussed by various Karen organizations and parties, and following the cessation of acute warfare, there is an atmosphere of positive change in the Karen region (Saw Thein Myint 2013).

One explanation for this historic breakthrough is that it is connected to an ambitious infrastructure project involving a SEZ and deep-sea port in Dawei. The project is part of a plan to connect with the Bangkok region via a new road and a pipeline serving as a short cut to avoid the time-consuming route through the Strait of Malacca. The road and the pipeline, however, cross Karen-controlled territory and, without a reliable peace process, neither the construction nor the use of the passage would have been possible. It is assumed that the KNU was pushed into ceasefire negotiations by the Myanmar and the Thai governments, which both consider this project highly important for future development. The Myanmar government was able to draw on the successful incorporation of various Karen groups into the political reform process. Moreover, during recent years the Burmese military was able to achieve small but continuous successes against the KNU due to its brutal "Four Cuts" anti-insurgency strategy (Smith 1999). Thailand was also in a powerful bargaining position over the KNU since it had tolerated KNU operations inside the refugee camps for a long time. This pressure aside, however, it seems that the KNU bought into the project with the promise of a share of the coming economic gains (Saw Kapi 2012; Saw Yan Naing and Kyaw Kha 2013). Following the logic of earlier ceasefire agreements negotiated by Khin Nyunt with various ethnic groups in the 1990s, the ceasefire with the KNU comprised administrative as well as economic guarantees. The extent to which this peace process will be sustainable has yet to be seen but the immediate consequence is that the civil war has ended and direct violent expulsions as well as casualties have ceased.

Although the fighting is over, the civil war has not only displaced people on a great scale but has created a new reality on the ground. Much of the farmland is either inaccessible because of landmines or is now being used for other commercial or infrastructural purposes. These fundamental problems have not been addressed systematically in the ceasefire agreement. On the contrary, now that the KNU has been co-opted into new economic projects on the Myanmar side (the Dawei and other infrastructure and SEZ projects), people are still exposed to evictions but under different circumstances. The expulsion by different means seems to make it increasingly difficult for people to return.

Moreover, in the course of the last twenty years people have lost their old lives. What happened was a de facto local integration, both into the local communities as well as into the camp situation. People have developed long-term strategies of survival and adapted to their specific camp situation and its permeability, or moved to other parts of Thailand. It is certainly true that the refugees are no longer farmers; they have been educated in Karen and English but not in Burmese, and even if they could return to their land they could not easily take up an agrarian way of life again.

The military *coup d'état* in Thailand

In Thailand too, a dramatic development has led to far-reaching changes in the border region. Following demonstrations in Bangkok, the military seized power on May 22nd, 2014 and ousted the administration of Yingluck Shinawatra who had been elected with a vast majority in 2011. The demonstrations that triggered the *coup d'état* were initiated by a conservative-royalist network known as the Yellow Shirts. Since the previous elections in 2005, 2007 and 2011 proved that the Yellow camp is in the minority, the organizers of the demonstrations resorted to nationalistic and xenophobic rhetoric for the sake of mobilization. The Cambodian government cooperated closely with former Prime Minister Thaksin Shinawatra and allowed the Red Shirt movement supporting Thaksin to operate on Cambodian territory, and so Cambodians in particular were targeted as a threat to Thai security. Immediately after the coup, it is said that 200,000 Cambodian migrant workers fled to their home country amid rumors that the junta had launched a crackdown. Migrants from Myanmar were not directly targeted by the populist mobilizations but the xenophobic atmosphere also reached the Thai-Myanmar borderland in the first half of 2014. The exodus, however, led to severe problems for the production sites relying on cheap migrant labor.

Operating under the name of National Council for Peace and Order (NCOP), the military has set up an administration and claims to pursue constitutional and administrative reforms to stabilize the country (*Mass Communication Organization of Thailand*, November 4, 2014). Although the NCPO had initially promised to hold elections in 2015, recent announcements suggest that plans to return to electoral democracy have been postponed indefinitely. This is why the new regime now struggles with a lack of legitimacy and seeks to prove its competence and effectiveness through a number of policies designed to bolster the flagging economy and cope with security questions. First, the military government embraced large-scale infrastructure projects, including projects on the Thai as well as the Myanmar side of the Thai-Myanmar borderland. Newly revived support for the stagnating SEZ in Dawei has to be seen in this light, since it promises to be an investment for the long-term growth of the Thai economy. Moreover, at their meeting in October 2014, Prime Minister Prayut proposed to President Thein Sein to set up a twinning project connecting production sites in Tak province on the Thai side and Myawaddy Province on the Myanmar side.

Second, the government is seeking to gain legitimacy by showing a strong hand in security issues including the question of so-called illegal migrant workers and refugees from Myanmar (*Bangkok Post*, October 10, 2014). This issue gained importance for the Thai junta especially after the US downgraded Thailand and Qatar on the human trafficking watch list shortly after the coup (Hodal, Kelly, and Roberts 2014). The policy of the strong hand was quickly translated into national policy: Two months after the coup, and as a reaction to both the mass exodus of Cambodian migrant workers and criticism from the US, the chairman of the National Council for Peace and Order's committee on migrant worker issues announced the establishment of so-called one-stop service centers where registration and preliminary recognition as a migrant worker could be obtained within 30 min. According to the new rules, a process of national verification has to be completed in cooperation with the authorities of the relevant country within two months. By April 2015, these offices had been established nationwide (National News Bureau of Thailand 2015). In the same vein, health schemes were broadened and registered migrants got access to health benefits comparable to the Universal Coverage Scheme for Thai nationals (*The Nation*, June 6, 2015). Parallel to the new infrastructure to help workers to register, the government increased raids on illegal workers in various parts of the country (cf. Kyaw Kha 2014; *Eleven Myanmar*, March 3, 2015).

Third, following the meeting between President Thein Sein and Prime Minister Prayuth, the Thai junta decided to dissolve the refugee camps along the border. Various institutions that had formed the backbone of the refugee regime had already decided to phase out the resettlement program from 2012 on. Now the Thai junta positioned itself at the top of the decision makers and announced that it wanted to repatriate all refugees in the near future (Saw Yan Naing, July, 2014). In preparation for this, the Thai authorities started a registration process inside the camps to verify residents' nationalities. As another option, the authorities also considered offering camp residents so-called "hill-tribe" ID cards allowing them to leave the camp to find work. Such a colored ID card, however, does not grant equal rights like a citizenship ID or registration as a migrant worker would.

The policy of the Thai junta thus led to a situation where the two groups, refugees and migrant workers, were recast, yet a hierarchical stratification of more or less legal migrants, who enjoy different rights, was left intact. After xenophobic agitation and rumors about crackdowns led to a mass exodus of unregistered Cambodian migrant workers and an immediate shortage of cheap labor in the whole country, the junta combined the establishment of SEZs as sites of exception exempted from minimum wage regulations with an active policy of registration, national verification, and access to social services, in order to staff the SEZs with cheap labor. This recast the potentially dangerous "illegal" migrant workers as legal – but due to SEZ regulations – equally cheap workers. At the same time, a new group of illegal migrants or second-class migrants were created, i.e. all those who cannot complete the national verification process after registration because they have lost their documents due to civil war or because they belong to the Rohingya and are not eligible for citizenship of Myanmar. A second group are all those who cannot be verified in the refugee camps and are given second-class "hill-tribe" ID cards.

Conclusion

It had been assumed that, with new governance strategies what has been construed as the central problems of the two groups of Burmese in Mae Sot – the regularization of migrant workers and the future of refugees – would be solved. However, the dynamics that are currently unfolding point in a different direction and reveal the constructed nature of the two regimes as well as the complex, contested and contradictory interests underlying the processes that constitute and govern the borderland. The case of the two migration regimes and the historical and actor-centered perspective we have chosen reveals the dynamics and mobilities that constitute and structure this specific borderland. In recent decades especially, political as well as economic interests have influenced the "doing of borders" and changed the borderland as well as the possibilities for mobile people. As described, however, neither the governance of the borderland by state authorities, which was and is accompanied by the categorization of mobile people, nor the economic global and national interests that also structure this space go unchallenged. The movements of people within the borderland can be interpreted as a contestation of state authority there. Despite the fact that the borderland is an example par excellence of the provincialization of global capital flows and reassertion of the political processes that are highly influential in doing borders, they also have to respond to mobilities. To analyze processes in the borderland thus implies not defining movements as exceptional but as an intrinsic aspect of borderlands, which leads to different forms of governance, landscapes of power, and new inequalities.

Acknowledgements

The authors wish to express their gratitude for valuable comments from the participants of the 4th Conference of the Asian Borderlands Research Network 8–10 December 2014, Hong Kong as well as to the two anonymous reviewers.

Notes

1. The empirical data consists of observations and formal and informal interviews the authors conducted, in cooperation with the Faculty of Political Science of Chulalongkorn University, with various representatives of migrant organizations, NGOs working with migrants and refu-

gees, institutions and government organizations in charge of migration and border control, and migrants and refugees themselves during a field trip in the border region in spring 2012. In addition to this, the findings of several other research projects by graduate and postgraduate students from a working group at the Department of Development Studies at the University of Vienna (including field studies inside refugee camps, and interviews with migrant workers and refugees on their expectations concerning resettlement) provide the background against which we analyze and discuss recent changes and dynamics in the border area.
2. The data was presented and discussed, among other occasions, on a joint panel at the International Conference of International Relations and Development (ICIRD) at Chulalongkorn University, Bangkok in September 2013. We are grateful to the Asian Research Center on Migration, especially Prof. Supang Chantanvanich and Prof. Naruemon Thabchumpon, for their valuable comments.
3. The question of whether to use the name "Burma" or "Myanmar" is highly contested. In this paper, we use Burma for the times before the country was renamed in 1989. Along the same lines, we use "Siam" instead of "Thailand" for the times before 1939. As for the population, we use "Burmese" or "Myanmar" as terms without ethnic specification. Where ethnicity is discussed, we use "Burman", "Karen", "Kachin", etc. However, throughout the paper, we do not imply any political message in this terminology. The decision to use "Karen" instead of "Kayin" follows the most established usage in Anglo-Saxon academic publications.
4. Lee (2011, 85) states for example that in 2000 40,000 Myanmar workers were registered only in Mae Sot, while around 200,000 lived in the area.
5. Thanks to Stefanie Kron for her valuable comments.
6. Although numerous refugees will have appreciated the possibility of being resettled in Canada, the US or a Scandinavian country, resettlement programs were actually unpopular on both sides. The governments of the destination countries had to justify the quota of immigrants but, as we will discuss below, even these quotas could often not be filled because refugees preferred for various reasons to stay in the border region.

References

Arnold, Dennis. 2013. "Burmese Social Movements in Exile: Labour, Migration and Democracy." In *Social Activism in Southeast Asia*, edited by Michele Ford, 89–103. London: Routledge.

Bowles, Edith. 1998. "From Village to Camp: Refugee Camp Life in Transition on the Thai-Burma Border." *Forced Migration Review* no. 2: 11–14.

Callahan, Mary P. 2003. *Making Enemies: War and State Building in Burma*. Ithaca: Cornell University Press.

Callahan, Mary P. 2007. *Political Authority in Burma's Ethnic Minority States: Devolution, Occupation, and Coexistance*. Washington: East-West Center.

Chan, Yuk Wah. 2013. *Vietnamese-Chinese Relationships at the Borderlands: Trade, Tourism and Cultural Politics*. London: Routledge.

Cheesman, Nick, Monique Skidmore, and Trevor Wilson, eds. 2010. *Ruling Myanmar: From Cyclone Nargis to National Elections*. Singapore: Institute of Southeast Asian Studies.

Cheesman, Nick, Monique Skidmore, and Trevor Wilson, eds. 2012. *Myanmar's Transition: Openings, Obstacles and Opportunities*. Singapore: Institute of Southeast Asian Studies.

Cunningham, Hilary, and Josiah Heyman. 2004. "Introduction: Mobilities and Enclosures at Borders." *Identities* 11 (3): 289–302. doi:10.1080/10702890490493509.

Dannecker, Petra. 2012. "The Changing Rural Landscape in Bangladesh Through Return Migration." *Trialog* 109 (2): 9–14.

Eberle, Meghan. L., and Ian Holliday. 2011. "Precarity and Political Immobilisation: Migrants from Burma in Chiang Mai, Thailand." *Journal of Contemporary Asia* 41 (3): 371–392. doi:10.1080/00472336.2011.582709.

Effner, Henning. 2013. *Myanmars Reformprozess. Eine Bestandsaufnahme.* Kuala Lumpur: Friedrich Ebert Stiftung. Accessed July 12, 2016. http://www.fes.de/international/asien/inhalt/burma.htm

Gupta, Akhil, and James Ferguson. 1992. "Beyond 'Culture': Space, Identity, and the Politics of Difference." *Cultural Anthropology* 7 (1): 6–23.

Hess, Sabine, and Vassilis Tsianos. 2007. "Die Autonomie der Migration." In *Turbulente Ränder. Neue Perspektiven auf Migration an den Grenzen Europas*, edited by Transit Migration Forschungsgruppe, 243–264. Bielefeld: Transcript.

Hodal, Kate, Annie Kelly, and Dan Roberts. 2014. "US Demotes Thailand and Qatar for Abysmal Human Trafficking Records." *The Guardian*, June 20. Accessed July 12, 2016. http://www.theguardian.com/global-development/2014/jun/20/thailand-qatar-downgraded-human-trafficking-report

Holliday, Ian. 2014. "Addressing Myanmar's Citizenship Crisis." *Journal of Contemporary Asia* 44 (3): 404–421. doi:10.1080/00472336.2013.877957.

Horstmann, Alexander. 2011a. "Sacred Spaces of Karen Refugees and Humanitarian Aid Across the Thailand-Burma Border." *Austrian Journal of South-East Asian Studies* 4 (2): 254–271. doi:10.4232/10.ASEAS-4.2-4.

Horstmann, Alexander. 2011b. "Borderlands and Border Studies in South-East Asia." *Austrian Journal of South-East Asian Studies* 4 (2): 203–214. doi:10.4232/10.ASEAS-4.2-1.

Horstmann, Alexander. 2012. "Stretching the Border: Confinement and Mobility Among Baptist Karen Refugees Across the Thailand-Myanmar Border." *Journal of Borderland Studies* 29 (1): 47–61. doi:10.1080/08865655.2014.892692.

Integrated Regional Information Networks (IRIN). 2013. *Myanmar-Thailand: Burmese migrant workers risk deportation.* Integrated Regional Information Networks. Accessed July 12, 2016. http://www.irinnews.org/report/96346/

International Labour Organization (ILO). 2015. *Review of the Effectiveness of the MOUs in Managing Labour Migration Between Thailand and Neighbouring Countries. Tripartite Action to Protect the Rights of Migrant Workers within and from the Greater Mekong Subregion (GMS TRIANGLE project).* International Labour Organization, Regional Office for Asia and the Pacific. Accessed July 12, 2016. http://www.ilo.org/wcmsp5/groups/public/--asia/--ro-bangkok/documents/publication/wcms_356542.pdf

Karakayali, Serhat, and Vassilis Tsianos. 2007. "Movements that Matter." In *Turbulente Ränder. Neue Perspektiven auf Migration an den Grenzen Europas*, edited by Transit Migration Forschungsgruppe, 7–17. Bielefeld: Transcript.

Kaur, Amarjit. 2010. "Labour Migration in Southeast Asia: Migrant Policies, Labour Exploitation and Regulation." *Journal of the Asia Pacific Economy* 15 (1): 6–19. doi:10.1080/13547860903488195.

Kyaw Kha. 2014. "Burmese Migrants, Thai Recruiters Arrested in Mae Sot." The Irrawaddy, September 25, 2014. Accessed July 12, 2016. http://www.irrawaddy.com/burma/burmese-migrants-thai-recruiters-arrested-mae-sot.html

Lee, Sang Kook. 2007. *Integrating Others: A Study of a Border System in the Thailand-Burma Borderland.* Doctoral Thesis. Singapore: National University of Singapore.

Lee, Sang Kook. 2011. "Borderland Dynamics in Mae Sot, Thailand and the Pursuit of the Bangkok Dream and Resettlement." *Asian and Pacific Migration Journal* 20 (1): 79–99. doi:10.1177/011719681102000104.

Li, Chenyang. 2012. "China–Myanmar Comprehensive Strategic Cooperative Partnership: A Regional Threat?" *Journal of Current Southeast Asian Affairs* 31 (1): 53–72.

Maung Shwe, Thomas. 2011. "Mae Sot soon to be Thailand-Burma Special Economic Zone." *Mizzima*, April 9, 2011. Accessed July 12, 2016. http://www.mizzima.com/business/investment/5156-mae-sot-soon-to-be-thailand-burma-special-economic-zone

Maung Thawnghmung, Ardeth. 2012. *The 'Other' Karen in Myanmar. Ethnic Minorities and the Struggle without Arms.* Lanham: Lexington.

Meehan, Patrick. 2011. "Drugs, Insurgency and State-building in Burma: Why the Drugs Trade is Central to Burma's Changing Political Order." *Journal of Southeast Asian Studies* 42 (3): 376–404. doi:10.1017/S002246341100033.

Migrants Assistance Programme Foundation. 2013. *March 2013 Migrant Registration Figures*. Thailand: Migrants Assistance Programme Foundation (MAP) Foundation. Accessed July 12, 2016. http://www.mapfoundationcm.org/eng/index.php?option=com_content&view=article&id=114:migrant-registration-figures-march-2013&catid=48&Itemid=79

Mintz, Sidney W. 1998. "The Localization of Anthropological Practice: From Area Studies to Transnationalism." *Critique of Anthropology* 18 (2): 117–113. doi:10.1177/0308275X9801800201.

Moe, Kyaw Zwa. 2012. "Mae Sot's Sudden Role Reversal." *The Irrawaddy*, May 11, 2012. Accessed June 28, 2013. http://www.irrawaddy.org/archives/4017

Myat Mon. 2010. "Burmese Labour Migration into Thailand: Governance of Migration and Rights." *Journal of the Asia Pacific Economy* 15 (1): 33–44. doi:10.1080/13547860903488211.

Naruemon Thabchumpon, Carl Middleton, and Zaw Aung. 2012. "Development, Democracy, and Human Security in Myanmar: A Case Study of the Dawei Special Economic Zone." Paper Presented at the International Conference on International Relations and Development (ICIRD), Chiangmai University, 26–27 July 2012.

Ong, Aihwa. 1999. *Flexible Citizenship: The Cultural Logics of Transnationality*. Durham: Duke University Press.

Ong, Aihwa. 2006. *Neoliberalism as Exception*. Mutation in Citizenship and Sovereignty. Durham and London: Duke University Press.

Ong, Aihwa. 2007. "Neoliberalism as Mobile Technology." *Transactions of the Institute of British Geographers,* no. 32: 3–8. doi:10.1111/j.1475-5661.2007.00234.x.

Pearson, Ruth, and Kyoko Kusakabe. 2012. *Thailand's Hidden Workforce*. London: ZED Books.

Pollock, Jackie. 2005. "Die Lebensqualität von Migrant/innen in Thailand." *Asienforum*, no. 26: 57–64.

Pollock, Jackie. 2013. "Migrants and Labour Day." *7 Day Daily,* May 1, 2013. Accessed July 12, 2016. http://www.mapfoundationcm.org/eng/index.php?option=com_content&view=article&id=115:migrants-and-labour-day-article-by-jackie-pollock-published-in-burmese-in-7-day-daily-burmese-and-english-versions&catid=38:articles&Itemid=65

Pongsawat, Pitch. 2007. "Border Partial Citizenship, Border Towns, and Thai-Myanmar Cross-Border Development: Case Studies at the Thai Border Towns." PhD diss., University of California.

Saw Kapi. 2012. "The Economic Forces at Work Behind the Karen Ceasefire." *The Irrawaddy*, April 11, 2012. Accessed July 12, 2016. http://www.irrawaddy.org/archives/2401

Saw Thein Myint. 2013. "Burma's Major Karen Political Parties Join Together to Discuss the KNU's Peace Talks." *Karen News*, March 29. Accessed July 12, 2016. http://karennews.org/2012/03/burmas-major-karen-political-parties-join-together-to-discuss-the-knus-peace-talks.html/

Saw Yan Naing, and Kyaw Kha. 2013. "Govt Grants Car Licenses to KNU, Other Ethnic Rebels". *The Irrawaddy*, May 27. Accessed July 12, 2016. http://www.irrawaddy.org/archives/35543

Schaffar, Wolfram. 2008. "Birma: gescheiterter Staat oder (neue) Form peripherer Staatlichkeit [Burma: Failed State or (New) Form of Statehood in the Periphery]." *Journal für Entwicklungspolitik (JEP), Austrian, Journal of Development Studies* 24 (2): 33–62.

Schearf, Daniel. 2013. "Thailand Extends Migrant Worker Registration Deadline." *The Voice of America*, January 18. Accessed July 12, 2016. http://www.voanews.com/content/thailand-extends-migrant-worker-registration-deadline/1586395.html

Scott, James. 2010. *The Art of Not Being Governed: An Anarchist History of Upland Southeast Asian*. New York, NY: New Haven.

Slodkowski, Antoni. 2012. "How Japan Inc. Stole a March on Competitors to Enter Myanmar." *The Myanmar Times,* October 8. Accessed July 12, 2016. http://www.mmtimes.com/index.php/business/2256-how-japan-inc-stole-a-march-on-competitors-to-enter-myanmar.html?limitstart=0

Smith, Martin. 1999. *Burma. Insurgency and the Politics of Ethnicity*. London: Zed Books.

Soe Lin Aung. 2014. "The Friction of Cartography: On the Politics of Space and Mobility Among Migrant Communities in the Thai-Burma Borderland." *Journal of Borderland Studies* 29 (1): 23–46. doi:10.1080/08865655.2014.892691.

South, Ashley. 2008. *Ethnic Politics in Burma. States of Conflict.* London: Routledge.

South, Ashley. 2011. *Burma's Longest War. Autonomy of the Karen Conflict.* Amsterdam: Transnational Institute/Burma Centre Netherlands. Accessed July 12, 2016. http://www.ashleysouth.co.uk/files/TNI-BurmasLongestWar.pdf

Sun, Yun. 2012. "China's Strategic Misjudgement on Myanmar." *Journal of Current Southeast Asian Affairs* 31 (1): 73–96.

Sutter, Robert. 2012. "Myanmar in Contemporary Chinese Foreign Policy – Strengthening Common Ground, Managing Differences." *Journal of Current Southeast Asian Affairs* 31 (1): 29–51.

Tan, Danielle. 2012. "'Small Is Beautiful': Lessons from Laos for the Study of Chinese Overseas." *Journal of Current Chinese Affairs* 41 (2): 61–94.

Thompson, Sally. 2008. "Community-based Camp Management." *Forced Migration Review*, 30: 26–28. Accessed July 13, 2016. http://www.fmreview.org/sites/fmr/files/FMRdownloads/en/FMRpdfs/FMR30/26-28.pdf

Thornton, Phil. 2006. *Restless Souls: Rebels, Refugees, Medics and Misfits on the Thai-Burma Border.* Bangkok: Asia Books.

Thongchai Winichakul. 1994. *Siam Mapped: A History of the Geo-body of a Nation.* Honolulu: University of Hawaii Press.

Walter, Susanne. 2012. *Invited but Not (Always) Willing to Go. Refugees in Tham Hin Camp (Thailand) as an Example of Migration Theories' Shortcomings.* Diploma Thesis, University of Vienna.

Weng, Lawi. 2012. "Rights Groups Say Migrants Blocked from Leaving Mae Sot." *The Irrawaddy*, October 2, 2012. Accessed July 12, 2016. http://www.irrawaddy.org/archives/15590

Woods, Kevin. 2011. "Ceasefire Capitalism: Military–Private Partnerships, Resource Concessions and Military–State Building in the Burma–China Borderlands". *The Journal of Peasant Studies* 38 (4): 747–770. doi. 10.1080/03066150.2011.607699.

Wyatt, David. 2004. *Thailand. A Short History.* Chiang Mai: Silkworm Books.

Zaw Aung. 2010. *Burmese Labor Rights Protection in Mae Sot.* Bangkok: Center for Development Studies, Chulalongkorn University.

Zaw Oo, and Win Min. 2007. *Assessing Burma's Ceasefire Accord.* Washington: East-West Center.

Newspaper Articles

"Borwornsak Uwanno to chair Constitution Drafting Committee." *MCOT.net (Mass Communication Organization of Thailand)*, November 4, 2014. Accessed July 12, 2016. http://www.mcot.net/site/content?id=54589668be047065fb8b461f#.VIPezzGUeSo

"Burma Government Signs Ceasefire With Karen Rebels." *BBC News Asia*, January 12, 2012. Accessed July 12, 2016. http://www.bbc.co.uk/news/world-asia-16523691

"Cross-border Economic Zone Plan." *The Nation*, 3 June 2012. Accessed July 12, 2016. http://www.nationmultimedia.com/national/Cross-border-economic-zone-plan-30183396.html

"Foreign Investment Jumps Fivefold in Burma." *The Irrawaddy*, May 13, 2013. Accessed July 12, 2016. http://www.irrawaddy.org/archives/34427

"Link Mae Sot to Other Projects, Pisanu Says." *The Bangkok Post*, June 13, 2013. Accessed July 12, 2016. http://www.bangkokpost.com/news/asia/354812/link-mae-sot-to-other-projects-pisanu-says

"Mae Sot Trade Zone Gets the Nod." *The Bangkok Post*, January 21, 2013. Accessed June 28, 2013. http://bangkokpost.com/news/local/331918/mae-sot-trade-zone-gets-the-nod

"Migrant Workers in Thailand Return Home as Arrests Increase." *Eleven Myanmar*, July 12, 2016. Accessed June 16, 2015. http://www.elevenmyanmar.com/local/migrant-workers-thailand-return-home-arrests-increase

"Migrants from Four Countries Eligible for Health Benefits." *The Nation*, June 6, 2015. Accessed July 12, 2016. http://www.nationmultimedia.com/national/Migrants-from-four-countries-eligible-for-health-b-30257469.html

"One-stop Service Opens Nationwide for Migrant Workers Today." *National News Bureau of Thailand*, April 1, 2015. Accessed July 12, 2016. http://thainews.prd.go.th/CenterWeb/NewsEN/NewsDetail?NT01_NewsID=WNSOC5804010010032#sthash.gVIuQsg0.dpuf

"Prayut tightens border controls" *Bangkok Post*, 10 October 2014. Accessed July 12, 2016. http://www.bangkokpost.com/news/social/436849/prayut-tightens-border-controls

"Second Mae Sot-Myawaddy Bridge Site Chosen." *Mizzima News*, 28 August 28, 2012. Accessed July 12, 2016. http://www.mizzima.com/news/inside-burma/7861-second-mae-sot-myawaddy-bridge-site-chosen.html

"Thailand, Myanmar to Twin Provinces." *Bangkok Post*, October 9, 2014. Accessed July 12, 2016. http://www.bangkokpost.com/news/social/436601/thailand-myanmar-to-twin-provinces

Mongla and the borderland politics of Myanmar

Tharaphi Than

Ceasefire agreements between the Myanmar government and different armed groups in 1989 created a new political map of the Myanmar borderlands. Once called black or brown regions because of their instability, border towns in the frontier areas, particularly in the Kachin and Shan States, became Special Regions. Unlike other border towns in Southeast Asia, where the state makes concession with a newly emerged global hegemon, China, old warlords in Mongla negotiate business transactions over dams, rubber plantations, and casinos with Chinese businessmen from Yunnan, Macau, or Hong Kong. And unlike other border towns where border crossing is at the discretion of an immigration officer, Mongla has no administration of border crossing and exchange of goods by any governing bodies. This situation is underpinned by a fragile relationship between the government and old warlords, a regular feature of border towns in north, north-eastern, and eastern Burma.

Background of Myanmar's Special Regions and Mongla

In Myanmar, one of the characteristics of the military regime[1] that came to power after the "failed"[2] uprising in 1988 is the emergence of Special Regions, the Myanmar equivalent of autonomous zones, in what was previously known as frontier areas during the British colonial era. Between 1989 and 1999, the military regime signed ceasefire agreements with 26 armed groups nationwide – from Kachin State in the north to Karen State in the south, and 13 of them were granted Special Regions status (see, e.g., Than [2015, 131-156] on the names of these groups and newly-created Special Regions). Mongla, locally known as Mai La (or La region), was one such region (142) (See Figure 1). It was granted an autonomous status, and it became Eastern Shan State Special Region 4 or in short, SR4 in 1989.

When the ceasefire agreement was signed on the 30th of June 1989 between the Burmese government and the National Democratic Alliance Army (NDAA) led by Sai Lin, Mongla became the headquarters of the latter. NDAA had 3300 soldiers in its army then.[3] An unknown town along the Myanmar-China border became the home of one of the warlords, Sai Lin, and the headquarters of his army. Special Regions are a gesture of the central government showing that they recognize the power and authority of ethnic leaders over their regions, even though their political regions or boundaries do not often reflect their regions' ethnic identity(ies) or mix. For example, the leader of the Special Region 4 is a Shan,[4] but the area he oversees is dominated by Akha, Lwe, and Lahu. The status of Special Regions indicates which groups wield the bargaining power with the government when the Communist Party of Burma (CPB) collapsed, and who came

BORDERLANDS IN EAST AND SOUTHEAST ASIA

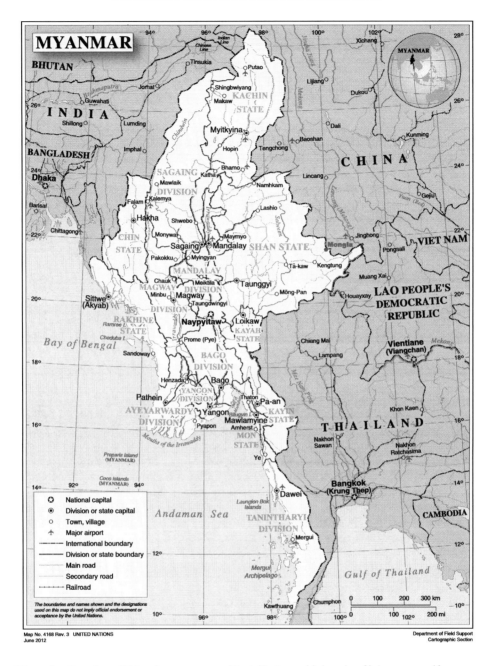

Figure 1. Location of Mongla. www.un.org/Depts/Cartographic/map/profile/myanmar.pdf.

to the ceasefire negotiating tables first. The Special Region status does not reflect the power – both political and cultural – of major ethnic groups in the borderlands. Just as with the mandate system after the Second World War, winners after the collapse of CPB, i.e. leaders of KoKang, Wa and their allies, divided up the frontier areas and started governing them as quasi-heads of state without necessarily representing the major ethnic group under their governance.

Border towns have assumed the titles of SR 1, 2, 3, etc., signifying the changing status of once insurgent groups who have now become autonomous administrations that oversee their own regions' economy and politics. New Special Regions not only signify the emergence of new powers but they also help draw a new politico-ethnic map for different ceasefire groups. While chieftains, individual inhabitants be they farmers, miners, slat traders, or immigrants from Yunnan, negotiated over resources, identity, and tax payments to the centers in the mountainous regions along the Myanmar-China border in the past, these negotiations and economic transactions have now been institutionalized, though not completely, via the operations of Special Regions after the central government's ceasefire agreements with the former warlords. Whereas in the past, locals might interact with both government agencies and rebel groups, the current arrangement with the Special Regions allows locals to see the Special Region as a proxy of the government as evidenced by visible state symbols and landmarks in these regions including state-sponsored pagodas. In other words, individual everyday engagement with the authorities and negotiations for economic opportunities have been formalized and institutionalized in the form of Special Regions (for economic activities on contraband goods, see Chang 2013). How these Special Regions have been managing their economies will be discussed in later sections of this paper.

Mongla, the heartland of Special Region 4, which is the topic of this paper, is situated 88 km north of Keng Tong in the Eastern Shan State of Myanmar. Its closest neighbour, Keng Tong, has been under the tutelage of Myanmar Kings since the sixteenth century. While Keng Tong is known in the existing literature as the last frontier town during the reign of the Myanmar kings, Mongla's identity as a town is less clear (see Than Tun [2004, 21-63] for more on Keng Tong). Studies of Yunnan and the China and Myanmar borders (Chang 2009, 2013; Ma 2013, 2014) provide a non-state centered analysis of how inhabitants in mountainous regions of Yunnan and Yunnan traders resist the administrative outreach of state bureaucracies, fleeing the state or incorporated state agencies, as in the case of the Lahu or Luohei minority. The Mongla region and the Akha minority there was not featured in these earlier insightful studies of the China-Myanmar borderland. At best, it is a backwater of both Myanmar and China, where only a small hamlet of houses existed before the area emerged as a Special Region. It is important to note here that Mongla until 2014 has not had its own ethnic identity unlike neighboring towns such as Keng Tong where Shan Sawbwas (hereditary chieftains) or aristocratic families ruled over their own minorities, and residents have had long ties and loyalty to their Shan leaders.

Unlike residents of neighbouring Keng Tong, where most proudly identify themselves as Shans or other varieties of Shan ethnicity such as Taing Ne, Mongla residents do not have a strong ethnic identity. Mongla as a frontier town also never posed political risks to either Myanmar Kings or Shan Sawbwas, who were often tributaries of the former. Unlike Northern and Southern Shan States, Eastern Shan State, where Mongla is located, did not pose a credible threat to the government. The government did not include Eastern Shan State as one of the insurgent hotspots that the army had to pay attention to (National Archives 1952).

In terms of geographical significance, Mongla exists as a shadow of its neighbour, Keng Tong, and in terms of political and ethnic significance, Mongla or Special Region 4 is generally seen as a little brother of two other groups in its vicinity, i.e. Wa and KoKang. But in 2014 SR4 leaders began demanding their own Akha region (SHAN 2014), an attempt that could be interpreted as a growing confidence of the SR4 leaders to not only reinforce their autonomy but also to distinguish themselves from other minorities such as Shan and Wa. The new Akha autonomous region will reflect the independence of SR4 – politically and culturally – from the Burmese-dominated government and the cultural hegemony of the larger groups in their locality. But the emergence of SR4 is always associated with the late 1980s and early 1990s ceasefire agreements between the government and rebels, and Mongla region is overshadowed by SR4 leaders' past history with armed conflicts and opium. In other words, the new name, Akha autonomous region, will not help SR4 get rid of its past tarnished image. Akha ethnic identity has been politicized over the struggle of SR4 for legitimacy as other ethnic identities such as Lahu or Luohei have been politicized over the struggle for resources like salt, tea or farmland (Ma 2013).

Challenges of and approaches to Myanmar borderlands studies

Mongla poses many challenges to outsiders – both tourists and scholars alike – just to travel there. From nearby Keng Tong, one can hire a private taxi individually or with other passengers to go there, since there is no public transportation. There are three check points between Keng Tong and Mongla; the first one is manned by the government, the second by joint forces (government and SR4), and the third one by the SR4 troops.

Like other Special Regions in the north and northeast of Myanmar, Mongla operates as a country within a country with its own time zone and currency, i.e. China time and *renminbi*. Located within the bounds of Myanmar territorially, it is closer to China linguistically and even culturally (Than 2015, 142-144). And Chinese from across the border have easier access to Mongla than Myanmar nationals, since one will have to pass through three check points from the Myanmar side before entering Mongla, whereas Chinese tourists can just cross the border illegally without having to pass through border gates or check points after the official border gate was closed in 2013.

A border region like Mongla could today be seen as a state within a state where different sovereign bodies (the Myanmar and Chinese governments and the SR4 government or administration) intersect and where different cultural hegemonies influence one another, but only after the regional conflicts ceased. In this report, recently renewed conflicts between the government and former ceasefire groups will not be discussed. Post-nation-state or post-colonial-ideologies and frameworks cannot explain the dynamics and development of a place like Mongla, in that unlike neighbouring Keng Tong, administrative and other organs of nation-states, or pre-nation-states, hardly reached Mongla. Nor was it part of the larger highland politics that neighboring towns were subject to (Shan federalism is a case in point); nor was it affected by post-cold war politics (unlike neighbouring Pang Sang, which was at the center of a China-US proxy cold war on Burmese soil).

Post-conflict Mongla has witnessed the processes through which the town and the people were brought into the modern state; people voted in the 2008 referendum, a standing Buddha image was built on the top of the highest hill to remind the people of the state religion, and a drug eradication museum reminds people of the success of the new Myanmar state that brought Mongla both national and international attention. Borderlands such as Mongla or SR4 can best be understood in the context of civil war or within the framework of post-conflict studies.

The region could also be a ground to test recent anthropological theories on borderlands as a site of contestation between *Mandala* and *Zomia* or center/lowlands and peripheral/highlands, and how state-non state alliances are built through illegal activities in this region (Chan 2013; Walker 1999; van Schendel 2002). To better understand what he called the *Zomia* region, where state formation has often failed, Schendel (2002, 647-668) proposes the flow of goods such as arms and opium as a tool of analysis instead of using state or area as the unit of analysis. Mongla is clearly a strong candidate for such an analysis, since it is located at the intersection of transnational drug flow. Walker (1999) conducted a field study in Laos to understand how boat operators and traders negotiate with different state authorities, engage in trading using many different currencies, and take advantage of the ambiguities that state borders present. Chan (2013, 89-106) posits that various stakeholders at the border – from residents to immigration officers – partake in regulatory practices in manning the borders, and shows how the recent development of the casino economy along the Vietnam-China border opens a new debate on borderland security involving post-reform China. Nyiri (2012, 533-562) contends that the emergence of China as a global power in the post-Mao era could also shed light on understanding the development of towns along the China-Myanmar borders as the economy is often fuelled by Chinese companies and tourists, and for Mongla, gambling Chinese tourists.

But unlike other Southeast Asian towns such as Golden Boten City in Laos and Lao Cai along the Vietnam-China border in which the Lao and Vietnamese governments have made business concessions to Chinese corporations which in turn have developed casino empires (Chan 2013; Nyiri 2012), Mongla remain an exception rather than the norm. The state did not intervene or manage the region here. In fact it is the autonomous state or SR4 administration that has granted business opportunities to Chinese companies and individuals. The emergence of China as a global power and China as a beacon of modernity (as opposed to Myanmar) underpins the characteristics of Mongla as a town where shop fronts proudly display Chinese signage, people talk on Chinese mobile phones, business is conducted in Chinese Yuan, and the whole town runs on China Standard Time (Than 2015). Nyiri called such an influence of China and Chinese culture and language in border towns a "synesthetic trick" (2015, 556), but in Mongla, it is not a trick, since those displaying Chinese styles and practising Chinese culture there are not local Shans, Akhas, or Lahus. They are indeed Chinese from China, mostly from Yunnan, who reside in Mongla on a temporary resident card. They are just extending their lifestyles and familiarities in life beyond the borders of China to Mongla on the Myanmar side. When I visited the town for the second time in 2014, Chinese had spread further inland, beyond the second gate (from the Mongla side), whereas during my first visit in 2013, their settlement stopped at the first gate. A Burmese with no Chinese language skills may simply be lost there.

As Rozenberg (1995, 159-176) explained in her article on the development and evolution of the tourist industry on the Balearic Islands in Spain, expectations from and interactions with tourists change the identity of a place. Mongla is no exception. Chinese tourists from Yunnan and neighboring provinces that are attracted to the casinos in Mongla help change the identity of the town and the ways in which the SR4 administration develop their region. The SR4 administration incorporated features that would attract Chinese tourists and appropriated cultures and services that their customers are accustomed to. In fact, Mongla could be seen as a poor Chinese's Macau; one could just cross the border – even illegally since the official border crossing is closed – and enjoy the gambling, sex, and exotic food that this Burmese Macau can offer (Than 2015).

As will be explained later in this report, the Mongla government's or SR4's reliance on their army to protect their autonomous status makes it necessary for them to generate their own income. And the SR4 administration found the casino economy to be a viable model for themselves; they seem to have borrowed the same model from other Special Regions and border towns such as Pang Sang under SR2.

Borderland studies of Myanmar are under-developed, and one should wonder whether it is feasible at all to embark on such studies if one does not have access to gate-keepers of the region and its information. In recent years, only journalistic accounts of Mongla have been published, and there exist no academic articles entirely on Mongla. For logistical reasons and safety concerns, Mongla is off the travel map for Myanmar nationals from within their country. I visited Mongla in 2013 and 2014 only for a few days. While visiting Kunming in China, I met two SR4 government administrative staff who have families there, and through their arrangement, I was able to visit the town for the first time in 2013 from Yangon via Keng Tong. During my first visit, I was able to meet a few low-level staff as well as Chinese NGO personnel and ask them questions. I was treated as a guest and taken to places by the staff. For a researcher, it was impossible to conduct independent research or observe the dynamic of the town and people and their daily activities without being chaperoned by the staff. In 2014, I made an unannounced day trip, via Keng Tong as in 2013. From these two visits, during which I had limited access to first-hand information from the people living and working there, as well as the archival research conducted at the National Archives of Yangon, I was able to understand the borderlands politics and casino economy of Mongla. I present preliminary findings on borderlands politics from these visits in this report.

The relationship between the Mongla SR4 administration and the central government(s)

Previously classified documents of the Burma Socialist Program Party (BSPP) indicate that the Socialist government's paramount concern in Shan State was the movements of the CPB, the Communist Party of Burma, and its allies such as the Wa army in and out of the government-controlled towns, as well as the trafficking of opium through the borders (National Archives 1982). The central government had very little political control over major border towns in Shan State. For example, in Muse, one of the biggest border trading posts in Northern Shan State, all 68 village tracts in the area were classified as either black or brown, indicating there was no political stability. The government provided only minimum services in these areas, and for the 80,000 people in Muse township, there was only one 16-bed hospital. The government army together with the 90-member strong People's Volunteer Army (Pyithu Sit) was in charge of the township security, and three full-time government firemen aided by three summer-time firemen paid by the town were in charge of emergency services (National Archives 1982, 34-38). Such limited government services and meager state spending in important border towns such as Muse highlighted how other smaller border towns such as Mongla were completely excluded from the government's border development plans during the socialist era.

But all this changed after the ceasefire agreements in 1989. The then-government, the State Law and Order Restoration Council (SLORC), declared that it would bring development to the "long-forgotten, war-torn, CBP-dominated, opium-growing" frontier areas, and Eastern Shan State was the first priority alongside Kachin, Kokang, and Wa (TGPP (Taing Gyo Pyu Pyu) [Historical Records of the State Projects of SLORC] 1991, vol. 1, 45). Various commodities from fertilizer to jeeps were sent to these regions, and the residents now had access to medical care at the newly-built government hospitals, veterinarians for their farm animals, and even funds to sculpt Buddha images. Development schemes were implemented in areas once considered brown or black. Mongla was regularly featured as a success story of the government peace process and drug eradication programs.

SR4 previously viewed the production of opium as a "historical necessity,"[5] but the region was declared drug free in April 1997. The government's two-pronged approach – to maintain peace and eradicate opium through development projects – seems to have worked. Mongla benefited from the Eastern Shan State development schemes, the third biggest in the government's development plans. But government aid was not enough to maintain peace in the Special Regions. For the ceasefire groups, their armies, not development, were the guarantors of peace, and they had to generate their own income to continually strengthen their armies. For this reason alone, the government's development schemes in the frontier areas, particularly in ceasefire regions, could never become a powerful tool to win the hearts and minds of the local people who still do not trust the central government.

In fact, one of the big brothers of the SR4 region, Kokang, fell to the government in 2014 after a second confrontation with government troops (Than 2015, 145-147). As much as the central government has wanted to claim the Special Regions as one of their own, and the development plans implemented there as the genuine efforts of the state to lift people out of poverty and "backwardness" (TGPP (Taing Gyo Pyu Pyu) [Historical Records of the State Projects of SLORC] 1991, vol 1, 15), leaders of the Special Regions, including SR4, do not trust the government. The Myanmar government, on the other hand, did not sustain their development plans launched in 1989, right after the ceasefire agreements. Once Buddha images were erected on mountaintops, hospitals built, and roads paved, the government plans ceased. And when localized confrontations broke out, the government pulled their services back – doctors were recalled, for example. This meant that the Special Regions have had to find funds not only to maintain their armies but also to continue with the development plans the government initiated.

The borderlands economy and casinos

Its strategic location as a gateway to China is one of the main reasons for Mongla to have become a major tourist destination for Chinese visitors, many of whom are illegal border-crossers. Leiper, who studies relations between gambling and tourism, posits that "proximity to a political border with a neighbouring country or province that outlaws casinos can be a factor behind the success of tourist destinations offering gambling facilities" (1989, 269). Mongla, which is under the jurisdiction of neither Myanmar nor China but that of SR4, fits this criterion.

Mongla, once the backwater of Myanmar and China, now hosts international visitors, including UN representatives who came in the early and mid-2000s to applaud the success of the drug-eradication programmes the SR4 administration had undertaken. Mongla's trajectory has been remarkable; a small town has transformed itself in a decade from a no man's land to a popular destination for gamblers. If it were not for the ceasefire and the casinos, Mongla is likely to have remained a forgotten frontier with porous borders and few attractions for Myanmar and China. Locals survive on subsistence farming and foraging, and Shan visitors from nearby towns only visit when the Akha and Lahu minorities of Mongla celebrate pagoda festivals, during which they display their cultures and traditions.

Not only Mongla's strategic geo-political location between Burma and China, but also its precarious relations with both states, can explain why casinos have become the engine behind Mongla's economy.[6] When casinos were opened a few years after the ceasefire agreement, Mongla was included in features with titles such as "Burma's City of Lights" (Williams 2003) and "Gambling on Law Lessness" [sic] in media for exiles such as *Irrawaddy* (Boot 2007). Casinos brought global fame to Mongla; or rather, casinos linked Mongla to global networks of vice. Not only gambling but also other entertainment such as transvestite shows attracted outsiders, including media attention, to the town (Than 2015, 142).

Mongla's rise as a gambling destination, particularly for Chinese visitors, was made possible by a collective strategy of border towns to generate their own revenues, mainly to sustain their armies and administer their own regions. SR4 administrative staff told me that owners of the casinos included Malaysians and Chinese, and one told me that the wife of SR4 leader Sai Lin, took an active interest in the casino business because of the amount of tax the industry generates. But none of the SR4 staff could give me the exact number of casinos in operation or the amount of revenue SR4 generates from them every year. Nyiri has linked Huang Mingxuan, a Hong Kong resident originally from southern Fujian Province in China, and Zhao Wei, a Macau resident, to casinos in Mongla (2012, 536-540). Both of them later moved their gambling empires to Laos.

Besides casinos, since 1989 Mongla leaders have built their own hydropower and coal power plants, constructed inter-village and inter-town roads, and supported farmers growing cash crops. Mongla leaders claim that in 2013 alone, they spent US$23 million on roads and bridges,[7] an amount most central regions of Myanmar could not afford. The question then is how an administration with a population of over 80,000 in an area of 4953 square kilometres can generate millions of dollars in a region with no industries and no previous history of food surplus.

The central government's track record in supporting the SR4 region is dismal, and this explains why SR4 and other Special Regions see casinos as reliable cash-generating schemes and incorporate them as part of their survival strategy. Mongla was first listed on the various projects of the Border Areas and National Races and Development Affairs Ministry as a priority site for literacy campaigns. Later, Italian companies such as Trevi were consulted for large-scale irrigation and construction projects (TGPP (Taing Gyo Pyu Pyu) [Historical Records of the State Projects of SLORC] 1991, vol 1), but none of the government records suggest that any work actually took place.

The government's development aid will never be enough for SR4 leaders and residents. The government supported businesses run by the ceasefire groups, granted them special privileges such as licenses for mobile phones as well as to buy diesel fuel and oil, and made concessions for gem mines. Development projects are designed to win the hearts and minds of the locals, and special privileges are granted to the leaders to continually secure their allegiance to the central government. However, the national budget does not match the greatest need of the leaders of the Special Regions, i.e. to maintain their armies; casinos therefore became a solution adopted by many leaders of the Special Regions to propel their economic engines. Even though the SR4 administration has claimed that the region now relies on its rubber plantations and cash-crops, and the leaders are asking for more support from the central government, it is reasonable to assume that the SR4 government relies on its casino economy to support many different projects within their own region, including strengthening their army.

In a place like Mongla the demarcation between what is legal and what is not becomes blurred. The central government does not have jurisdiction over Mongla, and while gambling is illegal in Myanmar, Special Regions are the exception. Leaders of these Special Regions set their own rules and the central government cannot intervene. There is no police station[8] and no postal service run by the government in Mongla.[9] Just like the Dork Niw Kham (Golden Niw Flower) in the Lao part of the Golden Triangle (Lyttleton and Nyiri 2011), Mongla has its own border crossing points and the local administration can establish their own rules of border entry (or lack of such rules), making it possible for visitors to the area to come and leave as they please.

There is a strong parallel between Myanmar border town casinos and the Native American casinos in the United States. Native Americans view themselves and their reserves as a sovereign nation, and they do not want to subject themselves to the law and taxation principles of the different states in which they are located (McGowan 2008, 65-79). Just as different Native American tribes are concerned over whether they are truly sovereign or have become a legal entity under the federal government, and therefore are not being treated as equals (2008, 68), leaders of the Special Regions probably could not imagine themselves as being at the mercy of the administrators of the Ministry of Progress of Border Areas and National Races and Development Affairs and officials in the capital, Naypyidaw. However, unlike Native American tribes, Special Regions consider their armies to be crucial to their survival. Not only administering tax revenues but managing their armies is the rationale behind the building of casino "empires" on the borders ruled by the Special Regions' leaders.[10]

There exists no study comparing the Native American gambling sites and the Southeast Asian borderlands casinos, and it would be difficult and perhaps far-fetched to ask whether Southeast Asian border casinos borrowed the economic model from the Native American tribes. Border casinos are most likely a prototype of those in Macau. Even the names reflect the established gambling empires of Macau. McGowan suggests that, of the US$30 billion revenue created by commercial casinos in 2004 in the United States, US$20 billion came from Indian casinos (2008). However, studies such as "Do Casinos Cause Economic Growth?" by Walker and Jackson (2007) suggest that casinos most thrive and boost the state's revenue in places where nearby states do not legalize gambling, and they also suggest that the economic boost from casinos "appears to be relatively short-lived" (2007, 603-604). Revenue figures for the Myanmar casinos remain elusive, making it difficult to understand the economic viability of casinos in Myanmar borderlands.

While Burmese records from the late 1980s and 1990s are scarce, or almost nonexistent, new casino proposals could serve as a telescopic lens for past events in the borderlands. Namkham, a border town in Northern Burma, and its 2012 proposal for casinos suggests that a conglomeration of Myanmar companies, probably managed by ex-warlords, and Chinese companies proposed to develop 35,000 acres for highways, 5-star hotels, casinos, schools, banks, residential buildings, hospitals, and bridges in Namkham (Nadi 2012). For a town with a population of 107,009 in 2014 (Gov 2014, 33), such a scheme reflects city-expansion plans designed mostly to attract and accommodate the needs of visitors (i.e. foreigners, be they Chinese or Thai). Chinese companies were chosen probably because of their wealth.

However, arguing that the concept and operation of borderland casinos have been influenced by Chinese capital and what the British colonial administration termed "agents of vice" of the Chinese has its own pitfalls (see Li Yi 2011 and Chan 2013 for discussions of Chinese and gambling). Historically, Shan State and its residents have not been shielded from the attractions of gambling. In fact, the British administration allowed and encouraged local gambling practices, especially during Durbar meetings in

Figure 2. Official border-crossing gate, which is no longer in use. Photograph by Tharaphi Than.

which the administrators and civil servants gathered together. Local heads of the different provinces granted gambling licenses to the highest bidders, and local games such as "Twelve Animals Top," which is similar to the Chinese gambling game of "Fish, Shrimp, and Crab," were major attractions of the festival that was held alongside these Durbar meetings. Both local officers and the British administration benefitted from gambling taxes.

Shan State therefore has a long-running tradition of using gambling as a reliable source of revenue for its leaders, especially in the border areas such as Mongla and Wa, where human and technical resources are lacking, and where commercial ventures are likely to fail. Many businesses in the UWSP-controlled Wa region, including a cigarette factory, paper mill, light factory, and beer brewery, have failed (Kramer 2007, 27). Bureaucratic procedures, and import and export taxes of the Myanmar and Chinese governments have compounded the woes of businesses, forcing the Special Regions to resort to businesses with little bureaucratic oversight and quick returns. Gambling businesses fit this criterion.

A CPB member and ex-interpreter between the Wa leaders and the Myanmar government during the ceasefire negotiations, who once had access to the leaders of different Special Regions (interview, July 2012), is critical of the Special Regions leaders. He does not believe that the casinos are the inevitable business choice for the borderlands governments. He argues that ever since the Communist Party of Burma began to allow its ethnic groups to engage in the opium trade following the China Communist Party terminating their support of the CPB in 1985, the genie has been out of the bottle.

Figure 3. Unofficial crossing gate. Behind this border demarcation stone, which says "Myanmar 1960," is a dilapidated fence, through which a hole has been cut for border crossers. Photograph by Tharaphi Than.

Witnessing and benefitting from the lucrative opium trade has left Special Regions leaders with little desire to engage in "traditional" trades in the development of their regions, *pace* Nyiri's argument that the casino economy could be seen as part of modernity and progress, and return from it could be pay-off for experimenting with contested sovereignty (2012, 557). More importantly, according to this ex-interpreter, the military remains the main pillar of the Wa, and possibly Mongla, administrations' regional and ethnic identity, and they need a steady supply of revenue to continuously strengthen their armies.

As to which Special Region first introduced casinos as a revenue-generating economic scheme is difficult to ascertain. What is known is that, by the late 1990s, almost all Special Regions, including the Northern Shan State Special Region under the control of the KoKang army,[11] the Northern Shan State Special Region (2) under the control of Chao Ngi Lai and Bao Youxiang, the Eastern Shan State Special Region (4) under Sai Lin, the Northern Shan State Special Region (4) under Say Htin, and Kachin State Special Region (1) under Zahkung Ting Ying,[12] were operating casinos in their regions. Other Southeast Asian border towns copied the model of Mongla (for example, Laos's Golden Boten City, Nyiri 2012).

Mongla, unlike other border towns such as Tachileik, is under no central authority's jurisdiction, making it possible for casino capitalists to build their empires and for gamblers (especially from across the border) to enjoy day or short-term visits. Until 2005, Chinese visitors could legally cross the border gate (see Figures 2 and 3 below) with temporary permits, but when the Yunnan government discovered some of its officials

Figure 4. Once the largest casino premises but now left in ruins. The signage reads 'Myanmar Royal Entertainment Company' and the lion statue resembles the guard lions usually built outside Burmese Buddhist temples. Photograph by Tharaphi Than.

pilfering state money, the gate was ordered closed by the Chinese government (Black and Fields 2006). Even though both the Myanmar government and, especially, the SR4 administration wish to reopen the border gate, to date the Chinese government has refused to give the green light. Many of the Chinese visitors to Mongla are therefore illegal border crossers, but their presence to this casino town is important and SR4 officials simply turn a blind eye to them, and to the illegal border gates and thief holes that are commonly known about in the town.

Figure 4 shows the façade of a casino in Wang Hseio, a 30-minute drive from downtown Mongla. The old casinos were left to rot when the Chinese government, or more probably the Yunnanese government, pressured the SR4 administration to close down the casinos. Instead of abandoning the casino economy altogether, the SR4 leaders decided to initiate a new casino town nearby (Than 2015, 147-148).

No photography is allowed inside casinos, partly to prevent live betting, which once thrived in Mongla casinos targeting Chinese. When I visited them in 2013, I saw only Chinese men and women of all ages including toddlers inside the halls. Most casinos are two-storied buildings, and their VIP rooms are located upstairs. Croupiers and other casino workers (see Figure 5) are local girls, and most seem under 18. One resident told me that since they could get jobs easily, they usually leave after primary school, attended Chinese language classes and landed jobs in casino halls (Than 2015, 147-148). Smoking is allowed inside the halls, and food and drink is available inside as well. Long couches were also seen near the entrance, where some people were sleeping,

Figure 5. Casino girls going to work, mini-markets and a gas station. Photograph by Tharaphi Than.

possibly gamblers taking a break. The halls are designed with full facilities including catering services, so that one does not have to leave the premises once inside. Slot machines were also found right outside the door.

The fall of opium production and the rise of the casino economy

The rise of casinos could also be explained by the success of drug eradication campaigns launched in the Special Regions in the 1990s. Because of his efforts in these campaigns, the United States removed the leader of SR4, Sai Lin, from their blacklist; not only the Myanmar government but also international organisations (including UNODC, the United Nations Office on Drugs and Crime) hailed the efforts of the SR4 administration for their eradication programmes (Khaw n.d). Nonetheless, UNODC recently admitted that the production of opium and ATS (Amphetamine type stimulants) in Myanmar has risen again (UNODC 2013); since 2007, opium production in Southeast Asia has been on the rise and Myanmar is no doubt responsible for this.[13] The Restoration Council of Shan State (RCSS) estimates that more than 300,000 Shan families grow poppies (Nyein 2013). Amidst these reports, my interviews with NGO staff in Mongla, as well as with SR4 administrative staff (Interviews 2013, 2014), reveal that opium is no longer grown, at least in and around Mongla, but that the production of ATS is on the rise.

One could argue that, given the situation with the central Myanmar government and international pressure, leaders of the Special Regions, including Mongla, cannot rely on the opium and drug trade as their main source of income. Casinos are a source of lucrative business for the leaders and their armies. The pressure on SR4 to continually strengthen their armies has grown since their ally, the KoKang army, fell in August 2009. One SR4 administrative officer commented in 2013 that they were on high alert. Casino businesses must continue in this fragile state. As for the Chinese government, as long as their officials are not involved, they will not intervene in the regular flow of illegal visitors to the entertainment city of Mongla. In fact, hotel construction is the second largest job-creating sector in Mongla.

The ex-interpreter to the warlord commented that "war and opium fuel each other" (Interview, July 2012). We can also substitute the word "opium" here with "ATS"; as long as the current Myanmar government and SR4 cannot trust each other, ATS production and the casino economy will continue to feature as prominent landmarks of Mongla and, for the same reasons, of other Special Regions as well. The same NGO official who had not seen a single opium plot in Mongla voiced the same position for ATS. However, he said that even ethnic villages are now witnessing a rise in drug addiction. In Mongla, both casinos and ATS production fuel the "state" economy.

In the case of Myanmar's Special Regions, casinos play an important role in the generation of revenues required by the region's leaders to sustain their armies, and arguably to develop their regions, thereby reinforcing their presence and dominance in the region as a legitimate ruler. In 2014, SR4 announced that they would demand the establishment of the Akha Self-administered Division, proving many commentators wrong by demonstrating that SR4, unlike the Kachin Independence Army, does indeed have strong political ambitions. According to the 2008 constitution, there are only six Self-administered Divisions, including the SR4 brother party UWSA controlling the Northern Shan State Special Region (2). No doubt economic prosperity in the SR4 region over the last two decades, and the continuous presence of the strong army, has boosted the confidence of the SR4 administration.

The SR4 administration imagines that, with the establishment of their own Akha Self-administered Division, locals' self-determination and awareness of their own ethnic and political identity will be strengthened. More importantly, the legacy of the Special Region, which resonates with war and opium trading, could also be buried in the ethnic-nationalism-provoking term "Akha Self-determination." This observation is echoed by Henders' argument that Macau's strong economy is key to explaining a declining state-centeredness, i.e. the role of the PRC in Macau's affairs (2001). Economic viability and political survival are closely intertwined in the case of the Special Regions. The strong economic performance of the casino businesses has enabled the SR4 leaders to request their own Akha Administration. Nevertheless, there remain serious social repercussions from their casino capitalism.

Social costs of casinos

As we have discussed, casinos are staffed by local youths. Many SR4 officials, by contrast, send their children to schools in Dalou and Jinhong, or even as far away as Kunming in China and Taunggyi, Mandalay and Yangon in Burma. One official has argued that, since young people in SR4 can easily obtain jobs at casinos with very low educational attainment, they are not interested in education, and parents cannot be persuaded to send their children to school beyond primary level. New employees at the casinos can expect to earn at least 1800 yuan or US$294, the equivalent of a professor's salary in Yangon. There is no reliable healthcare in Mongla. The rich travel to Mae Sai in

Thailand or Sipsongpanna in China for medical treatment and check-ups. The local school and hospital remain a symbolic presence of the central state, barely providing the essential services locals need.

Alongside casinos, brothels also operate in downtown Mongla. Before 2004, it is reported that Chinese girls from all over China came to work temporarily in Mongla, saving enough money to return to their hometowns to engage in ordinary livelihoods. Girls from northern China have now stopped coming, and one health official from the SR4 administration estimates the number of prostitutes to be no more than 200; these are mostly from Yunnan and the southern provinces of China. This is the number of prostitutes who are screened regularly by the SR4 health department. The number working outside the brothels, usually Myanmar girls, could be much higher, although it is difficult to verify the exact figure.

Conclusion

The casino economy in Special Region 4, Mongla, is a special form of "development," made possible by the ambiguous political and economic arrangements between three "states," i.e. Myanmar, China, and SR4. As long as the civil war continues in Myanmar, the warlords of the borderlands in Myanmar will continue to rely on the revenues from the casino economy for their armies. The changing political environment in the borderlands of Myanmar, particularly in the post-ceasefire era, engenders different political agencies (special regions and their armies), economic partners (casino empires and Chinese gamblers), and social agencies (ATS producers, brothels, prostitutes, card dealers). The continued instability and the fragile status of the borderlands in Myanmar will continue to affect the dynamic of these border regions.

Notes

1. The official name of the regime was the State Law and Order Restoration Council (SLORC), which was then changed to the State Peace and Development Council (SPDC).
2. The term is contentious, since some viewed the collapse of the 26-year rule of the Socialist Programme Party (BSPP) during the uprising as a victory in itself regardless of the coup d'etat that followed.
3. This information is based on figures presented on a panel located on the second floor of the Drugs Eradication Museum in Rangoon as of 2013.
4. There is no information on the ethnic composition of the SR4 administration.
5. Unpublished document, SR4, May 2013. I was given two document sets of eight pages each by an SR4 administrator when I visited the town in July 2013.
6. This argument is based largely on observations in the town and interviews with SR4 administrators. Official documents provided by the SR4 administration to the author in May 2013 do not include revenue figures, and there does not seem to exist any statistical data on the state of the economy in the SR4 region.
7. Documents provided by the SR4 government. These documents seem to have been produced by the government to hand out to visitors interested in the administration of the region. They include the amount of money the government has spent on roads and bridges, and the programs the government has undertaken, much like the front page of the central government's newspapers.
8. In fact the government's troops can be stationed only at the first of three security gates in the SR4 region, as earlier noted.
9. Only Chinese mobiles can be used inside Mongla but there is no signal in the casino site, Wang Hseio.
10. The 2009 KoKang incident, during which government troops launched attacks on KoKang and the Northern Shan State Special Region, ending their existence as an autonomous state,

11. The KoKang army collapsed following their 2009 fighting with the government. Some of the leaders and soldiers took refuge in SR4, as an SR4 administrator told me in June 2014.
12. These were the leaders when the Special Regions were first established in 1989.
13. Myanmar, after Afghanistan, is the world's second largest opium producer.

References

Black, M., and R. Fields. 2006. "Virtual Gambling in Myanmar's Drug Country." *Asia Times*, August 26.

Boot, W. 2007. "Gambling on Law Lessness" [sic] *Irrawaddy*. Accessed October 13, 2013. http://www2.irrawaddy.org/print_article.php?art_id=6632

Chan, Yuk Wah. 2013. *Vietnamese-Chinese Relationships at the Borderlands: Trade, Tourism and Cultural Politics*. London and New York: Routeledge.

Chang, Wen-Chin. 2009. "Venturing into "Barbarous" Regions: Transborder Trade among Migrant Yunnanese between Thailand and Burma, 1960s–1980s." *The Journal of Asian Studies* 68 (2): 543–572.

Chang, Wen-Chin. 2013. "The Everyday Politics of the Underground Trade in Burma by the Yunnanese Chinese since the Burmese Socialist Era." *Journal of Southeast Asian Studies* 44: 292–314. doi:10.1017/S0022463413000088.

Gov (The Republic of the Union of Myanmar). 2014. *Population and Housing Census of Myanmar, 2014*. vol. 1. Naypyidaw: Department of Population.

Henders, S. J. 2001. "So What If It's Not a Gamble?: Post-Westphalian Politics in Macau." *Pacific Affairs* 74 (3): 342–360.

Khaw, P. n.d. National Task. Ministry of Home Affairs: The Central Committee for Drug Use Control. Accessed August 17, 2013. http://www.ccdac.gov.mm/articles/article.cfm?id=420

Kramer, T. 2007. *Neither War Nor Peace: The Future of the Cease-Fire Agreements in Burma*. Amsterdam: Transnational Institute.

Leiper, N. 1989. "Geography of Tourism and Recreation." *GeoJournal* 19 (3): 269–275.

Li, Yi. 2011. "Local and Transnational Institutions in the Formation of Chinese Migrant Communities in Colonial Burma." PhD diss., University of London.

Lyttleton, C., and Pal Nyiri. 2011. "Dams, Casinos and Concessions: Chinese Megaprojects in Laos and Cambodia." In *Engineering Earth: Impact of Megaengineering Projects*. 3 vols, edited by Stanley D. Brunn, 1243–1266. Dordrecht: Springer.

Ma, Jianxiong. 2013. "Clustered Communities and Transportation Routes: The Wa Lands Neighboring the Lahu and the Dai on the Frontier." *Journal of Burma Studies* 17 (1): 81–119.

Ma, Jianxiong. 2014. "Salt and Revenue in Frontier Formation: State Mobilized Ethnic Politics in the Yunnan-Burma Borderland since the 1720s." *Modern Asian Studies* / FirstView Article, 1–33. doi:10.1017/S0026749X12000868.

McGowan, Richard A. 2008. *Historical Guides to Controversial Issues in America: The Gaming Debate*. Connecticut: Greenwood Press.

Nadi, N. M. 2012. "White Tiger Party Opposes Permission for Land Grant for Namkham Development." *DVB*. Accessed October 11, 2014. http://burmese.dvb.no/archives/24290

National Archives. 1952. *Military Strength and Their Locations up to February 1952*. [Previously classified document.] Yangon: National Archives Department. Document number 4/4 (21), Accession number 14536.

National Archives. 1982. *Report by the Autumn Operation Group 3, 3 February 1982*. Yangon: National Archives Department. Series Number 4118 (35), Access Number 39009.

Nyein, N. 2013. "Opium Eradication Agreements Lack Impact: Shan Rebels." *Irrawaddy*. Accessed August 20, 2013. http://www.irrawaddy.org/archives/42396/print/

Nyiri, Pal. 2012. "Enclaves of Improvement: Sovereignty and Developmentalism in the Special Zones of the Chna-Lao Borderlands." *Comparative Studies in Society and History* 54 (3): 533–562.

Rozenberg, Danielle. 1995. "International Tourism and Utopia: The Balearic Islands." In *International Tourism: Identity and Change*, edited by Francoise Lanfant, Marie-Françoise Lanfant, John B. Allcock, Edward M. Bruner, 159–176. California: Sage Publications.

van Schendel, Willem. 2002. "Geographies of Knowing, Geographies of Ignorance: Jumping Scale in Southeast Asia." *Environment and Planning D: Society and Space* 20 (6): 647–668.

SHAN (Shan Herald Agency for News). 2014, March 19. *Mongla to Call for Self Administered [Sic] Status*. Accessed January 23, 2016. http://english.panglong.org/mongla-to-call-for-self-administered-status/

TGPP (Taing Gyo Pyu Pyu) [Historical Records of the State Projects of SLORC]. 1991. 3 vols., Rangoon: SLORC historical records committee.

Than, Tharaphi. 2015. "Black Territory to Land of 'Paradise': The Changing Political and Social Landscape of Mongla." In *The Age of Asian Migration*. Vol. 2, edited by Yuk Wah Chan, 131–156. Newcastle upon Tyne: Cambridge Scholars Publishing.

Tun, Than. 2004. *Neh Hleh Yazawun, [Itinerant's History]*. 4th ed. Yangon: Pyeson.

UNODC. 2013. *Transnational Organized Crime in East Asia and the Pacific: A Threat Assessment*. UNODC.

Walker, Andrew. 1999. *The Legend of the Golden Boat: Regulation, Trade and Traders in the Borderlands of Laos, Thailand, Burma and China*. London: Curzon Press.

Walker, D. M., and J. D. Jackson. 2007. "Do Casinos Cause Economic Growth?" *American Journal of Economics and Sociology* 66 (3): 593–607.

Williams, J. 2003. "Mong La: Burma's City of Lights." *Irrawaddy* 11 (1). Accessed July 23, 2013. http://www2.irrawaddy.org/article.php?art_id=2806

"Trust facilitates business, but may also ruin it": the hazardous facets of Sino-Vietnamese border trade

Caroline Grillot

> This article focuses on the operational dynamic of informal small-scale trade in the Sino-Vietnamese borderlands as disclosed by local traders' strategies of negotiation. It questions the impact of financial transaction practices – management of official fees and procedures related to payments – on the sustainability of cross-border trade. It engages with the notion of "trust" and stresses its significance in a space where the vagaries of trade policies challenge business rules, and contest the local power hierarchy. It argues that despite the principles underlying "trustful cooperation" being unevenly adhered to, traders manage to adjust to one another's methods, revealing the nature of their tacit complicity in maintaining business logistics regardless of the limits imposed by national policies, institutional regulations and stereotypes.

Introduction

The trading cities of Móng Cái (Quang Ninh Province, Vietnam) and Dongxing (Guangxi Province, China) both constitute a cross-border economic cooperation district officially named the Dongxing-Móng Cái Free Trade Zone, a key strategic element of regional economic development and transnational integration in the Greater Mekong Subregion. Since there is great diversity among cross-border traders (Cheung 2000; Chan 2013), this article focuses on traders who operate small-scale businesses in the main Móng Cái market. These traders sell a diverse range of goods – clothes, electric appliances, medicine, etc. – and negotiate prices with their customers on a daily basis. I concentrate in particular on the critical perspective of established Chinese traders in Móng Cái who are smuggling their goods from China, and who have disclosed to me the operational dynamic of this informal trade. The analysis is based on data collected during three months of fieldwork in both Móng Cái and Dongxing, and a long-term familiarity with the Sino-Vietnamese borderland communities where I have conducted research projects regularly over the last ten years. After introducing the particular setting where Sino-Vietnamese border economic activities occur, I provide traders' insights into the strategies of negotiation. These insights question the impact of financial transaction practices, including management of the fees that frame business (rent, tax, shipping), and procedures related to payments for traded goods on the sustainability of cross-border trade. Drawing on ethnographic examples, the final section of this article engages with the key concept of trust in a Chinese context or *xinyong*. This stresses how central the issue of trust is in a space where the uncertainties and vagaries of trade and state policies challenge business ethics and rules, and contest the local power hierarchy. This article argues that despite the principles underlining "trustful cooperation" being unevenly adhered to, many traders do manage to overcome difficulties and adjust to one another's methods, and that the issue of "trust" must be considered against the background of growing economic development in this region.

The fragile balance of the border economy

Borderlands are often places of disorder regulated by informal rules and local interpretations of state regulations (Horstmann and Wadley 2006). In their *Companion to Border Studies*, Wilson and Donnan (2012, 17) draw on the recent scholarship on borders and propose to conceptualize them "as processes, as floating signifiers, as waypoints and conduits in the flow of peoples, ideas, goods, capital and threats to the body politic." In this context, licit trade and illicit activities all occur simultaneously and their nature changes according to variations of circumstances. As Abraham and van Schendel (2005, 7) remind us, "official rules, structures, and discourses do posit a sharp distinction between law and crime, but it is essential to understand that this claim is only one element in the nexus of practices bridging the licit/illicit divide." In spaces such as Móng Cái and Dongxing, such an understanding is embedded in all the local trade praxis. In order to introduce the setting, the following is an overview of the core issues that underline the atmosphere surrounding small-scale trade, as experienced and articulated by the agents directly involved in business operations.

Issues of stability and security constantly emerge from the narratives of Chinese traders either established in Móng Cái or conducting cross-border trade in the area. *Bu wending* [unstable] and *bu anquan* [insecure] are words they use to express their feelings towards the local environment they must cope with in order to organize their business activities. The perplexities and worries they depict indicate three levels of insecurity. The state level comes first. In recent decades, and particularly during the time when the research that informs this article was conducted (2013–2014), several episodes marked a vivid resurgence of the never-ending question of sovereignty over maritime territories that both China and Vietnam claim to be theirs. Although the venues of these disputes are a long way from Móng Cái and Dongxing, the border area and the traders themselves are affected by the states' regular emphasis on unsolved historical issues. Frictions at the diplomatic level, spread throughout media and propaganda materials, regularly arouse suspicion and paranoia among people who have difficulty maintaining a critical distance from the manner in which geopolitical matters are explained and represented. As Zhang Juan (2011, 312) emphasizes,

> [m]emory at the borderland is full of ambiguity; it is in a state of liminality that constantly vacillates between forgetfulness and remembrance. People by the border can never forget, nor fully remember, thereby dwelling at the edge of reminiscence as they strive forward.

In the borderlands, patriotism and nationalism always find a niche in which they can flourish among those eager to believe that the enemy is next door, precisely when frustrating everyday practices tend to provoke each other's distrust.

State propaganda maintains tension and provokes debates among locals, who see in any sudden strict implementation of regional policies and border trade rules the direct consequence of another diplomatic crisis. The instability of the geopolitical environment goes hand in hand with business precariousness. This is illustrated through unpredictable schedules of border controls, confiscation of merchandise, or feebleness and unreliability of business counterparts, some of the direct consequences of local authorities' decisions to follow the governmental guidelines and to tighten regulatory procedures. Operating businesses under such conditions undeniably creates a feeling of insecurity since traders and their direct logistical partners (paperwork negotiators and shippers) lose control over their activities, and the overall fluidity of trade dynamics. But delayed deliveries are not the only consequences of frontiers being overly scrutinized. Frozen food, for instance, gets directly affected by various delays on the shipping route. The extra expenses in electricity to keep the containers cold in border warehouses while waiting for permission to cross the border are at stake. Some transporters considered them to be too high of a risk for their budget and they sometimes sacrifice food security to increased storage costs, which may lead to freight abandonment. The anxiety created by the increasing instability of the diplomatic relationship and consequent variations in border management is also palpable in the local markets: closed shops, bored sellers, empty corridors, a lack of products, an inability to keep promises, and different disputes have recently been obvious signs of Chinese traders' discouragement.

But experienced traders know that diplomatic ups-and-downs only represent one side of the challenge in cross-border trade. Insecurity concerning the possibility of receiving goods from suppliers in China, and delivering them in time to Vietnamese clients also depends on the personal connections maintained by each trader, with business partners all along the shipping route, and on his/her capacity to overcome logistical difficulties so as to honor his/her contracts with customers. In terms of expenses, such exceptional arrangements may have consequences in terms of imposing additional financial pressure on already weakened traders. These costs include additional bribes to customs officers, border guards and market management employees. They also include extra investments in shipping through alternative routes organized by transporters and carriers who raise their prices in moments of diplomatic crisis inducing tightening control over border crossing; traders may find themselves exposed to various risks and subsequent penalties or crackdowns because of smuggling.

In Vietnam, Chinese people are aware that they attract little sympathy because of their dominating economic power. Even though not all of them believe in the Vietnamese military threat emphasized in Chinese propaganda discourse, they reportedly encounter acts of intimidation and various interferences in the regular processes of their business, including life threats, rendering them anxious and insecure. This is especially the case for those who lack the relevant connections to ease their everyday operations, and the capital to invest in bribes to deter harassment and those who face difficulties in the business project itself, independent of conjectural factors. This is the case for some Chinese traders who have established their wholesale shops in Móng Cái's Central Market, a place where the constant turnover of businesses indicates the difficulties many encounter in succeeding in a national market that requires constant adjustment.

There, the controversial management of trading spaces adds another layer of dissatisfaction to the general feeling of unease of Chinese wholesalers and shopkeepers. This constitutes the third level of insecurity. Business in Móng Cái's Central Market is conducted in large open spaces where shops are predominantly tiny and full of displayed wholesale products with a constant turnover. Business can be fast, especially in the morning when Vietnamese customers rush into the market to snap up good deals and organize shipments. In this quite chaotic dynamic, shop owners pay attention to every move (Figure 1). Experienced traders advised me of the existence of some very well organized thieves, who steal certain products with the presumed complicity of insiders.

Figure 1. Outside Móng Cái's Central Market, packaging Chinese commodities for shipping through Vietnam (Photograph by Caroline Grillot 2013).

Stories of the complicity of acquaintances involving interpreters or market security guards abound and motivate traders to remain extra cautious and to avoid leaving valuable items in their shops overnight. Hence, at night, despite the presence of night watchmen, metallic shop doors and shop door padlocks, all shopkeepers keep a private strongbox inside which they store valuable products (such as mobile phones, electronic devices and cash). Many also choose to take their money to China on a daily basis (albeit within the limited allowable amounts).

The logistics of border trade necessitate a close collaboration with Chinese and Vietnamese agents, in the private sector as well as the state sector. However, in this particular market, relationships with management officers are oftentimes sensitive to negotiate. Mr. Wu, a women's garments shopkeeper in the Central Market, describes his perplexity regarding official demands:

> Importing Chinese goods to Vietnam through official gates or smuggling channels exposes us to the payment of various shipping costs, including those paid to customs. But even after the goods arrive at the market, we must handle lots of other fees. In this market we pay different taxes: land tax, state tax, shop façade tax and management tax, and we also have various fees such as shop and storage rental, electricity, security, insurance (which we are forced to buy, for fear of seeing our shops destroyed by fire), and other occasional fees, such as for repairs (which are very high in terms of what they are paying for).

Each stallholder offered his/her own understanding of the variety of taxes collected in the market, and it became tricky to distinguish which of these applied to owners and which to renters of the stalls. Official figures were as difficult to obtain, and each market had its own management system. Three remarks were recurrent among Chinese traders: taxes they had to pay in order to enjoy a shop in a Vietnamese market space exceeded what they would pay in China for a similar setting; some occasional taxes were not quite "official"; and the visible outcome of the efforts made by taxpayers was non-existent or deemed as inadequate. Mr. Wu provides his perspective on market management:

> Market management tax supposedly contributes towards the protection of traders in the market during working hours, and overnight when the market is empty. This is a compulsory tax, and yet we don't feel protected. Fights often occur between customers and sellers, you know, about payments and returned goods most of the time. We call security if things turn violent, but no one appears. They are around but they choose not to react…until they feel things may get out of control. Then, they intervene to penalize the shopkeeper. Even if the customer is in the wrong, security usually protects them; then, if a Chinese trader complains or refuses to pay a fine for "disturbing the market," that trader's shop will be closed until he complies. Is this protecting us? I don't get it. They need our business to develop the city and provide Vietnam with affordable industrial goods, but their management only dissuades us from staying here. What's the benefit for the country?

Chinese traders generally live on the Chinese side of the border, for convenience and for safety reasons, as they see Vietnamese border cities as relatively insecure and backward in many senses. Allegations of regular armed robberies, the power of local mafia, and the corruption of local authorities prevent most Chinese from staying any longer than necessary each day in the Vietnamese borderland. Besides the environmental insecurity that underlies their articulation of a feeling of distrust, various aspects of trade-related activities act to sustain suspicion in the minds of Chinese traders. Maybe markets such as Móng Cái's Central Market are no less secure than similar market settings in China, but the flexibility and negotiation space within which they are able to resolve issues remains limited. This compels them to perceive their position as that of "victim" being abused by an unscrupulous and uncontrolled management. Issues of security constitute the ground on which business partners conduct negotiation, but here also mistrust tends to shape the exchanges and terms of agreements.

"A *Yuan* is a *Yuan*" – negotiating with the Vietnamese

In the context of market transactions, Vietnamese customers and their Chinese suppliers approach each other through the prism of an army of stereotypes related to their culture and their commercial ability. To ease exchanges and negotiations, most traders who do not speak their business partner's language rely on interpreters. Most interpreters are Vietnamese women who have learned Chinese, or who are of Chinese descent ("Hoa" – Chinese from Vietnam), i.e. well connected in business circles on both side of the border and very much aware of cultural differences (Hai 2000). With their assistance, during negotiation both parties also rely on empirical observation to evaluate the degree of trust and reliance they can expect from their partner or, as Mick Moore articulates it in his attempt to conceptualize "trust," their mutual "predispositions to act in a certain way" (1999, 76).

Comments from Chinese traders reveal that the problematic issue of trust is very much linked to the understanding of values such as honesty and loyalty. This is especially true for Chinese migrant traders who felt unrelated to Vietnamese by cultural or historical common references. They perceive their business partners solely through the lens of the economy, and rarely endeavor to ground their mutual understanding, and bond their relationship beyond the limits of their transactions of commodities versus money. All that matters to traders is the ability of their customers to fulfill the moral obligations embedded in business deals, including those that could facilitate and sustain the setting of a long-term partnership in the pursuit of common interests. For instance, Chinese traders often complain about the negotiation skills of their Vietnamese customers: "To the Vietnamese, a *yuan* is a *yuan*, they are very thrifty"; "They hardly concede anything, even when we are old partners"; and "They don't understand what loyalty means." For Chinese traders, appearing flexible and even generous during a negotiation is an implicit business rule. While Vietnamese traders do not want to appear greedy, their Chinese counterparts perceive this reluctance to engage in any commercial gesture as an absence of business skills.

A Qiu, a Vietnamese trader of Chinese origin (a Hoa), runs a sport items business in Móng Cái and has years of experience in cross-border trade and transcultural interaction. He describes the different mechanisms:

> Let us imagine a Chinese wholesaler who has a stock of clothes to sell. Each item cost him 5 yuan, including factory price and transportation cost, so he wants to sell each item for at least 10 yuan to make a good profit. He then sets his selling price at 10 yuan per item. Then a buyer comes and conducts a negotiation to get each item at a lower price than 10 yuan, while the seller tries to get an amount as close to 10 yuan as he can. Still, each party has a potential space of 5 yuan in which to bargain and reach an agreement. If they agree on 7 yuan, the buyer is satisfied (he lowered the initial price) and the seller makes a reasonable profit. But when a Vietnamese seller has goods to sell to a buyer, he acts differently. He directly sets a reasonable price rather than a highly profitable price. When asking for 7 or 8 yuan per item in the first place, he considers that this is already a good deal for him and for the buyer. The negotiation space is therefore very limited, and sometimes nonexistent. To Vietnamese traders, being too greedy does not represent an honest way in which to conduct business. They prefer to set a reasonable price to begin with and reach an agreement easily, so as to avoid the trouble of extended bargaining. In short, take it or leave it. On the contrary, a Chinese trader would rather negotiate and appear accommodating by conceding on a low price while in reality he has already made a significant profit.

In the above situation, when the original price of merchandise remains unknown, Chinese traders interpret the Vietnamese non-compromising attitude as an inability to conduct negotiation. To them, Vietnamese traders do not know how to bargain, are inflexible and are unable to adjust to their clients' expectations. They ignore the one basic rule of business: offer compromise to win the loyalty of new customers. However, Chinese traders provide two explanations for this behavior. Firstly, they attribute to Vietnamese people the inclination to be cunning and stingy, which interestingly is also attributed by Vietnamese to the Chinese (Endres 2015). Secondly, they refer to a delay in Vietnam's economic development, which anchors its people in a pre-liberalism mentality. "They act like Chinese people used to 20 or 30 years ago; they are inexperienced and do not know how to bargain" is a recurring comment heard among complainers. As condescending and simple as they may sound, these assumptions, among many other similar statements, show how different ways of dealing, especially when they are perceived as repetitive, can lead to widespread empirical accounts that translate annoyance and suspicion on both sides, and affect the mutual perception of business ethics and trust.

Another recurring issue linked to negotiation is the perilous way in which payments are made. Delayed payments and repeated indebtedness undermine the whole mechanism of small-scale trade and constantly put at risk both parties involved. From the Chinese point of view, this becomes a crucial issue in their endeavor to establish or maintain reliable partnerships and retain regular Vietnamese customers. One of the main issues here is that business negotiations occur and the terms of payments are set without any safety net, or as Peebles (2010, 232) puts it, without "a regulatory authority or a common bond of trust that enforces it," a "precondition [that] represents one way in which credit/debt brings together temporal and spatial regulation." The general practice is that customers do not pay cash on the spot. They order, pay a deposit, pick up the goods, and promise to pay later. Because business is based on trust, without any written contract, whatever is agreed on the phone or during a business meeting is expected not to be retracted. However, Chinese wholesalers claim that Vietnamese customers often do not pay their debts on time, in violation of their oral agreements. They find reasons to delay payments, and they sometimes simply disappear without discharging their debts. This contributes to the establishment of a hierarchy between debtors and creditors that actually places power with the Vietnamese. How and why? The method employed by Vietnamese customers (whether a retailer in Vietnam or an intermediary representing one or several retailers) is apparently easy.

For example, a Vietnamese customer (an intermediary, usually a woman) orders a certain quantity of an article at one garment shop where she has bought clothes previously, and so she and the wholesaler already know each other. She pays a deposit and, when the goods are delivered, she pays another portion of the total price. Indebting herself, she leaves with the stock of articles and promises to pay the outstanding portion later. When the due time arrives, or when she needs to visit the same shop again, she explains to the wholesaler that she needs more time because she does not have the money (for various reasons). To avoid trouble, she orders another stock of items on behalf of another source (an order for another retailer for instance), who is possibly more important (showing her appreciation of the shop's clothes choice), pays another deposit, and leaves with the goods, leaving behind another installment in addition to the initial debt.

She proceeds in such a way that the Chinese wholesaler has no choice but to accept her conditions. If he/she does not, he/she risks losing the initial investment (since it may remain unpaid indefinitely), while still having to pay the garment factory in China where the order was placed; in addition, the wholesaler could lose a client with whom he/she has already dealt and placed trust in. On the other hand, if he/she accepts, there is a risk of entering into an endless cycle of unpaid debts and half-kept promises. Upon being pressured, the Vietnamese customer may well pay the outstanding amount due from one debt earlier, but the wholesaler nevertheless remains indebted. In addition to these risks, she may simply choose to change her supplier.

Mr Han comes from Guangdong province (China) and has been selling loungewear in Móng Cái's Central Market for a decade. He speaks Vietnamese and is very knowledgeable about doing business in Vietnam. He offers an explanation:

> Vietnamese traders have little capital and so they need to invest and reinvest it without waiting for the benefit. This is why they pay for their orders with numerous small payments rather than one or two large ones. In the meantime, they can put the money towards another business deal if they feel there is better potential elsewhere. They adapt quickly. In many cases, the client of an intermediary also delays payments. It forces her to advance us the money for an order, in addition to shipment costs, which means she must indebt herself.

Hence, intermediaries sometimes disappear without clearing their bills. Intermediaries also demand unusual things such as exaggerating the amount of an invoice, so that they can make more money at the expense of their own customers in Vietnam. Even though I don't like to support such practices, I must comply if I don't want to lose a customer... These practices also exist in China but in different proportions. I would say that in China 20 percent of deals face similar issues while the figure is 80 percent in Vietnam.

It is important for Chinese wholesalers to have capital, to enable them to order new products and remain competitive in the business. Many emphasize how their customers were honest at the beginning of their partnership, and slowly took the liberty of imposing delays in payment, even when business ethics require that all due debts should be cleared at least once a year, prior to the New Lunar Year. Song, a Chinese entrepreneur from Jiangxi who recently invested his family savings in opening a small shop in Móng Cái market feels stuck:

I am unlucky with this business. Some clients are honest but many don't respect our agreement and always ask for delay in paying their debt. I don't like this place, but how can I leave without being paid? Every day, I look for them to come back. Sometimes they pay a little, find excuses, and promise that the rest will come soon. They sometimes make a new order. So I need to import new clothes, and I may attract new customers; otherwise I don't make any money. I can't spend my time waiting, and I can't chase after them, they have local connections... I can't stop now.

Newcomers recognized how they had started business partnerships successfully enough to feel confident. Their customers fulfilled their payment obligations and respected the agreed-upon contracts. Based on such experience, they often become more adventurous and make additional investments and choices. But when they begin to face irregular payments from some clients, those whom they trusted, they usually find themselves already in a delicate position that forces them to stay until they get paid; otherwise they would lose their investment. Meanwhile, in order to survive economically, they engage in other deals to either secure the fragile relationship established with their indebted client, or in hopes of entering into transactions with other reliable customers.

It is interesting to note that Chinese traders feel that Vietnamese business people do not share their values and business principles, ignoring in their assessment the fact that these principles face irregularities in China as well. Nevertheless, these practices in the art of negotiation put the Chinese traders in a very uncomfortable position, which not only worries them and disrupts their commercial strategies and long-term investment plans, but also deters them from considering their Vietnamese customers as sustainable and reliable business partners.

When one decides, out of necessity or as driven by structural conditions, to conduct business outside of the formal channels of import-export, one might expect to work with no safety net, as in any site of informal economy (Stammler-Gossmann 2012). Trade is conducted on the basis of reliable, longstanding contacts, unwritten contracts, and trust. As one of the problem areas relates to capital flow, prior to discussing the core issue of trust let us first explore the issue in another space: the patterns of financial transactions/exchanges in what I have labeled the "Móng Cái little Wall Street."

"Móng Cái little Wall Street": money transfer procedures

Exploring the financial modalities employed by Chinese and Vietnamese traders once they have reached a business agreement offers an alternative approach to the delicate concept of trust and distrust; a concept that is put at stake since it obviously affects daily cross-border interactions between communities, and feeds the challenge of implementing a national economic agenda at the ground level.

Most Chinese traders who arrive in Móng Cái and Dongxing have an ambition to engage in cross-border trade and raise money as quickly as possible. Pursuing this aim, however, they must deal with one important and pragmatic question: money transfer. For those engaged in import-export businesses, modalities of capital exchange may well be similar to those experienced during business operation in China, as long as they agree to pay the high fees charged by financial institutions in relation to currency exchange. For many traders who choose to avoid these troubles and expenses, including small-scale traders operating in the Móng Cái Central Market, an alternative option is to adopt another system. Understanding and adjusting to local everyday practices in terms of currency exchange, private banking and credit management is crucial to the implementation of the business projects of Chinese traders.

In the realm of small-scale trade, generally no contract is signed between a supplier and a customer. Each party simply maintains a record of orders in a well-kept notebook. Hence, word and trust constitute the sole basis of business deals: trust in the Chinese wholesalers' ability to supply the goods on time, with the expected quality at the agreed price and according to a regular logistical procedure; and trust that the Vietnamese customers will collect their orders, will pay according to the agreed-upon schedule and will refrain from changing their mind or returning unsold goods. Payment is of course the dominant link in this logistic, since each link in the commodity chain between a factory in China and a retailer in Vietnam requires some form of investment, and imposes responsibilities on the wholesalers and their shipping partners. At any time, there exists the potential that one of these links will fail to respect a contract and put at risk the business deals of many intermediaries. Money transactions are administered according to well-established rules that suppose an accurate evaluation of risk on the part of those who use informal banking systems.

In Móng Cái, this system is administered and controlled by a large group of Vietnamese women established inside the markets, on street corners and in the notorious currencies market that I have labeled "Móng Cái little Wall Street" (Xie 2000). If one wonders why women dominate the currency trade, people unanimously answer that Vietnamese men in general are very poor money managers and money wasters. As a consequence, women are usually in charge of the family budget and other money transactions such as private loans, lotteries, or underground banking systems. Those women operating in Móng Cái come from different backgrounds and generally work with regular customers who, once their deals have tested their mutual trust, may introduce new customers, following a snowball system. These women use their personal bank accounts in Vietnam to deposit and withdraw currencies according to their customers' needs. They make profit by lending capital without paperwork, charging an exchange/interest rate lower than in the bank; they raise their incomes by getting commissions. Both parties find the system efficient, fast and flexible. The currency exchange rates are adjusted daily, the interest rate is negotiable according to customers' situations, and all agreements are based on each party's word.

Van is one of the black-market money actors. She is a Vietnamese woman who lives in a common-law marriage with her Chinese husband in Dongxing. Originally the translator in her husband's electrical appliance shop, she decided to become a money-changer to sustain their family after the business went bankrupt. Although this new role allows her greater flexibility and more time, in addition to providing her with a higher income, risk constitutes a delicate aspect of her position. Every day, Van meets her customers either at their workplace (shops) or at her rented space in "Móng Cái's little Wall Street." There, in a basic open space simply covered by a roof, dozens of experienced moneychangers spend their day endlessly counting large amounts of cash. Seated on an elevated platform covered with a bamboo mat, each woman occupies approximately (Figure 2) one to two square meters, which is enough space to sets up a metallic box (locked), an electric fan, a calculator, a handy bill-counter, and a phone charger, as well as to sit and welcome customers. The intrusion of strangers (such as a foreigner) into this space is usually met with indifference and closed expressions on these women's faces: time is money, and operational confidentiality is the rule. This is where many cross-border traders, previously introduced by regular customers, exchange their cash into their neighbor's currency, eliminating the need to negotiate the regular banking process. Van explains how it works:

> The simplest way for a Vietnamese client to pay a Chinese wholesaler for instance is transacting the money via the bank account of a money-changer like me. In this case, I receive the due amount in đồng[1] (VND) in my account; I then withdraw it, change it into Chinese currency [according to the black market rate] and hand it in cash to the Chinese boss. Alternatively, I can deposit it into his Chinese account,[2] or make a transfer in *yuan* (RMB) from my own Chinese account to his. Usually each Chinese boss and Vietnamese client works together in association with one or several money-changers. We require trusting relationships, which take time to establish. In this type of transaction, I don't make a profit

Figure 2. The end of the day in "Móng Cái little Wall Street" (photograph by Caroline Grillot 2013).

by providing this service in itself, but I do make a profit when changing the money at the black market rate.

In appearance, the process seems easy although one may wonder why bother when it is legally possible for any Chinese or Vietnamese citizen to open a bank account in the neighboring country. Van reveals the interesting outcome of this procedure:

> The advantage is that, in the official financial system, there will be no visible connection between a buyer and a supplier. The only visible track of a transaction will be between the Vietnamese client and myself at the Vietnamese bank, and possibly between the Chinese wholesaler and myself at the Chinese bank. Such an easy transfer doesn't require any explanation at the bank. The transaction is simple, but if I agree to pay the whole amount in advance, I will actually lend money to the Vietnamese client, who will then need to reimburse me with rather high interest. That way, I can also make some benefit. Previously, interpreters also served as face-accounts for Chinese bosses but there were a few scandals involving interpreters who flew off with money from deals in their account. So now Chinese bosses prefer to make arrangements with professional moneychangers. It's a question of trust.

Therefore, the whole procedure is based on trust, that is, on the tacit acceptance of the money changer's financial conditions, and potential deception. However, in the end, according to my informants, this procedure remains cheaper than direct international bank transfers and guarantees the necessary invisibility of small-scale trade that relies mainly on smuggling: no track, no direct link between business partners, and no tax. How money changers manage to avoid controls resulting from the constant activity in their bank accounts remains uncertain; this is a matter that Van elides by simply stating that "banks are too busy with large financial transactions to care about our small money management." When she says "small," she is actually referring to a few tens of thousands of *yuan*. Van seems to insinuate that consequent bank transfers may become the subject of banks' scrutiny, although more investigation is required to support the idea of a differentiated degree of flexibility on the part of local bank regarding money flows.

Money flows are such that, when making a decision on a deal, all cross-border traders must find a balance between the absence of formal tracks and the consequent financial benefit of tax evasion on the one hand, and the risk of facing unscrupulous customers or go-betweens, with the potential subsequent loss of investment and stock, on the other hand. Relating to what Parry and Bloch remind us in their discussion on the concept of gift, money is not a neutral instrument; it also "contains and transmits the moral qualities of those who transact it" (Parry and Bloch 1989, 8). Street money traders, as well as their customers, have equal chances to find and bond with reliable business partners, although they may also fall into traps. But their sense of solidarity and their ability to communicate usually spread the news about bad payers. News of unfortunate endings to collaboration also prevents a trader who failed to honor a contract to find local trustworthy moneychangers, and this may seriously jeopardize his/her business as well. Trust is an invisible and hardly controllable factor in trade, especially cross-border trade, because one of the two actors of a deal can easily disappear into one's own country without fear of being investigated or followed. But disappearing might not imply going away. Several local traders informed me that when someone often changes his/her mobile phone number, it gives a warning. This person is trying to avoid being found and forced to face the consequences of previous trickeries. The system works well enough to allow the development of economic exchanges, but in general, mutual cautiousness remains the rule.

The "trust" capital

> "Trust is the trustfulness of a trustor: the extent to which the trustor is willing to take the risk of trust being abused by the trustee" (Buskens 2002, 8).

The notion of trust has been debated in many disciplines of social science, which have all approached it from different angles, without agreeing on any clear and definite definition that entails every dimension of what is, eventually, a presumption granted to an Other. However, in the introduction of her comprehensive review of trust-related literature, Barbara Misztal (1996) pointed out a few points that are enlightening in our understanding of the sensitive business relationships at stake in the Sino-Vietnamese border trade. First of all, trust is a social mechanism, or an instrument of social organization. But its impact can only be measureable on the long term: "the trust features… require a time lapse between one's expectations and the other's action" (1996, 18). And as our case study reveals, trust "always involves an element of risk resulting from our inability to monitor other's behavior, from our inability to have a complete knowledge about other people's motivations and, generally, from the contingency of social reality" (1996, 18). Such inability becomes exacerbated in a context of small-scale trade carried on without formal proper contracts, or reliance on legal tools that protect sellers and customers from various forms of abuse. Being a fundamental component of informal trade between Vietnamese and Chinese, trust remains nevertheless extremely difficult to negotiate along the routine of daily practices, even to Chinese traders known for the dynamism of their economic activities, and their efficiency regardless of their methods.

Many authors have studied the Chinese business system, and it is not the purpose of this article to explore its complexity further. Rather, it concentrates on the manner in which Chinese traders articulate the difficulties they encounter in Vietnam, especially when the business ethics on which they rely show their limitations within this challenging context, as well as their capacity to overcome such obstacles in their pursuance of commercial projects.

Barton (1977) conducted research among the Chinese community in southern Vietnam in the early 1970s, exploring the strategies and requirements on which their activities were grounded. He assessed the importance of the widely acknowledged notion in Chinese economics of *xinyong*. Chinese business practices build on the concept of *xinyong*, which the author defines as "the basis for a particular type of business strategy which emphasizes personal relations and the maximization of long term advantage" (Barton 1977, 150). *Xinyong* usually translates as "trust," but Tong (2014, 13, 14), analyzing the contemporary Chinese community of Singapore, also suggests that "*xinyong* should be translated as integrity or credibility or reputation and character of a person" and that *xinyong* is a "dynamic concept, a mode of adaptation for operating in particular historical and environmental conditions."

Chinese traders who operate in Móng Cái typically mention two spheres of interaction with Vietnamese where, according to their experience, the issue of *xinyong* becomes problematic, to a more consequential extent than is the case within the framework of their interaction with other Chinese: the negotiation process and the credit system. In the first sphere of interaction, as the examples above have shown, a trader seeks trust in his potential partner in order to establish a long-term business relationship. In the circle of Chinese traders, be they within China or among overseas communities, projections of future deals rely mostly on a delicate evaluation of *xinyong*. A potential new partner's behavior, words and actions are put to the test. According to Tong, the importance afforded to *xinyong*, and the preference of Chinese traders for oral agreements and contracts, particularly in a border context where a large proportion of small-scale trade uses informal channels, originates from a lack of trust in legal systems:

> Vis-à-vis this lack of systems trust (or systems distrust), Chinese traders came to rely on personal *trust* or *xinyong*, preferring to work with individuals whom they personally trusted and seeking to bring new acquaintances within their personal realm of familiarity. Much energy is invested in establishing and nurturing personal relations or *guanxi* and developing good *xinyong*, which is a personal property (Tong and Yong 2014, 57).

Since the early stage of the socialist-oriented market economy in Vietnam – the Đổi Mới policy implemented in 1986 – access to formal financial institutions has been difficult for most private entrepreneurs building up their own firms (McMillan and Woodruff 1998). Reliance on informal credit systems was observable two decades ago and is still considered as a preferred means of gaining access to start-up capital and investment funds. Trust is thus a fundamental value to cultivate and maintain, in addition to the avoidance of customers who renege on commitments. One possible method through which to measure the degree of trust a trader places in a customer is the level of credit granted. Consequently, as observed by McMillan and Woodruff in their research, one way for a customer to test his/her partner is to intentionally delay payment to increase the debt, in order to evaluate how much more credit he/she could gain without arousing suspicion and jeopardizing the trustful relationship (1998, 9). While such behavior (also noticeable in Móng Cái's market transactions) is understood as a testing tactic from the viewpoint of the Vietnamese customer, it is nevertheless easily misunderstood and may produce the opposite of the desired effect among Chinese traders. While several of my informants acknowledged that tolerating payment delay might be necessary, and over time it was possible to build up sufficient confidence in a customer to maintain an effective business partnership, many others felt profoundly disturbed and annoyed by this game. Obviously, the nature of border trade – unreliable, risky, and volatile (at least regarding small-scale trade) – places enormous pressure on traders, whose purpose is to quickly raise profits with immediately efficient deals, rather than working on establishing long-term partnerships with customers they sometimes barely know. The interactions that traders maintain with their various partners (suppliers, shippers, customers) are often limited to distant phone calls, and negotiation through mobile and slippery intermediaries.

The social distance that is inherent to the specific nature of some cross-border business partnerships complicates the reliance on such usual principles as the examination of reputation. Indeed, reputation is probably one primary way to measure trustworthiness (Tong 2014). However, here again, Móng Cái's market activities take place against a rather particular backdrop of actors' mobility that does not ease access to personal background. Both Chinese traders and Vietnamese customers deal with each other with the knowledge that, upon the occurrence of any dispute over goods quality, payment or delivery, the easiest way out of trouble is to vanish far from the border in one's own country, leaving no option for negotiation or retaliation.

Some behaviors act to provide an indication of a partner's reputation. Several experienced traders explained that, when a partner suddenly changes his/her phone number without notice, this means that he/she has reneged on a commitment, be it financial (debt, credit) or related to contract follow-ups. Another indicator is the period of time in which an individual has worked within a specialty, which can reveal a lack of ability to maintain a business, and sustain connections and partnerships, regardless of environment, crisis or financial difficulties. However, when Chinese traders are strict with Vietnamese customers who have failed to respect a contract, this may bring a bad reputation among their other local customers, hence threatening their business sustainability in a foreign environment.

In the way Chinese traders articulate the challenging behavior of their Vietnamese customers, mistrust may sometimes lead to charges of dishonesty. However, from a Vietnamese point of view, such business conduct should not be used to question the honesty of either party. Mr. Guan is a Vietnamese seafood dealer in Móng Cái. His Chinese family background allows him some analytic distance from which to view these financial movements:

> In our business field, we can't pay cash for daily transactions. That would be costly and unsustainable. Consequently we establish a credit system. We must sell the merchandise before being able to raise a profit, and then pay our bills. Chinese traders who can pay cash have a clear advantage over us. They have stronger financial means than we do. Such a system could not be implemented realistically in Vietnam, and so we must indebt ourselves and wait for an opportunistic moment to settle our debts. I myself use the bank to make more profit. I pay my suppliers [fishermen] once every two weeks. In the meantime, I deposit my profits in the bank so they can yield profits, and then later I pay my suppliers. So I make more profit than if I had paid them immediately after selling the fish to my customers. I see nothing wrong here.

When asked why their Vietnamese partners waited a relatively and variably long period before settling a bill, several traders and intermediaries, well informed in financial practices in Vietnam, also mentioned this procedure. They suggested that placing short-term investments in the bank produced sufficient financial interest to make this practice worth following. To some needy traders (in goods or currencies), the small profits made from this practice made it worth the risk of irritating their Chinese trading partners and jeopardizing the *xinyong* capital they have invested in their business contracts.

From the Chinese perspective, particularly for those who do not yet understand – or accept – the subtle financial mechanism at stake, delaying payment is actually interpreted as a means of forcing them to more flexible and tolerant than they would have been had their partner also been Chinese. From their standpoint, being tested is being controlled. "*Mei banfa* [there is no other way]" is a common answer to enquiries concerning the Chinese traders' manner of tackling recurrent difficulties with indebted clients reluctant to pay in good time. Patience, tolerance and adjustment to local practices are the end result of their helpless position, and this is especially the case for those who cannot afford to turn down customers, or turn to another business project, in a very competitive commercial environment.

While Chinese traders feel disrespected because their Vietnamese customers fail to act in accordance with Chinese business ethics, their Vietnamese counterparts believe their flexibility in terms of finance and operation is limited by structurally unbalanced trading conditions due to a rather different level of commercial development and experience. Misunderstandings and disagreements in practice lead both parties to nurture the conviction that the other deliberately and mutually abuses their position, resulting in frustration and a compulsive focus on the notion of trust as the sole explanation for the other's failure.

Conclusion

Despite its dynamics, the ongoing commercial activity in Móng Cái actually hides internal flaws of trade practices and consequent infringements to trustful partnership. New cohorts of traders keep replacing those who failed, and give the illusion that conducting sustainable business is also possible under informal economic conditions, that is to say, those based on trust rather than contract; but the issues remain. In line with recent ethnographies on credit and debt that have shown how the "credit/debt nexus is productive of social ties, allegiances, enmities, and hostilities" (Peebles 2010, 234), this article analyzes Sino-Vietnamese trading collaboration through the modalities of their financial transactions. It highlights that behind the complexities of maintaining trust between communities of traders, the ground that sustains their relationship of reciprocity is constantly renegotiated.

Meanwhile, scholarship on border trade between China and Vietnam often emphasizes how the complex and asymmetric historical relationship between these countries frames the nature of border community interactions. However, as Kirsten Endres (2015, 734) stresses in her account of small-scale traders in Lào Cai, another Vietnamese border town, the border

> emerges as a productive site, in providing not just access to economic opportunity but also a boundary through and across which identities are shaped. As complex, multidimensional processes that involve both short-lived interactions and carefully cultivated relationships with the neighborly Other, these borderland identities and alterities are continuously in the making.

Surely, such relationships are mirrored at the level of trust Chinese and Vietnamese traders accredit each other when they carry out their borderland activities. Chinese activities display the prosperous image of their nation's economic development, and their ambition to expand their power in the region. In response, unable to compete with the same resources of their neighbor, the Vietnamese often adopt a defensive behavior built on a strong ability to negotiate their resources under their own conditions.

Maintaining a reliable trustful relationship among trade's stakeholders is at the core of the development of economic cooperation. But according to Móng Cái's Chinese and Vietnamese cross-border traders, this still remains only a wish. Drawing from their experiences, traders elaborate a discourse on trade ethics as understood in Chinese and Vietnamese business cultures. This discourse is regularly raised as a safeguard against the breach of trust they believe they are frequently the victims of in the course of their business dealings.

However, one should not underestimate such practices as modalities of negotiation and financial transactions in small-scale trade – the ground for mutual benefits – in evaluating the capacity of Chinese and Vietnamese traders to eventually overcome structural difficulties, including cultural differences, in conducting business. While the Chinese traders may understand the Vietnamese methods as irregular and unethical when it comes to evaluating their working principles, they also enjoy some convenience, as in the case of money transfer procedures. The Vietnamese may keep a cautious attitude toward their Chinese suppliers by imposing their rules on their territories, but they benefit from a growing border-trade that compensates for the lack of industrial products made in Vietnam. In the pursuit of similar goals, traders' efforts to adjust to one another's methods reveal their degree of understanding, and the nature of their tacit complicity in their attempt to maintain their own business logistic regardless of the limits imposed by national policies, institutional regulations and stereotypes.

Current everyday practices suggest that the shadows of the past and remaining conflicts may not deeply affect the actors of cross-border trade. Chinese migrant traders, the largest group of business people who operate in Móng Cái markets nowadays, mostly come from outside the borderlands and do not necessarily relate to the specificities of local history. Their feelings of distrust towards their partners emerge from uneven commercial experiences, communication misunderstandings, rumors, competitive pressures, and culturally marked approaches to capital management, rather than from political rhetoric. Still, their mutual dependency eventually makes their partnership improve toward more stability despite discrepancies, making the development of border cities such as Móng Cái a "work in progress."

Acknowledgements

This article has greatly benefitted from constructive comments received at the 4th Conference of the Asian Borderlands Research Network, Hong Kong, City University of Hong Kong (December 2014) "Re-openings, Ruptures, and Relationships" (8–10th December, 2014). Special thanks go to the anonymous reviewers, and to my colleague Kirsten Endres for their valuable comments and suggestions on the earlier drafts. I am most grateful to the Institute of Cultural Studies (Vietnam Academy of Social Sciences, Hanoi) for their support, in particular to my research assistant Dinh My Linh for her patience, help and insights during fieldwork, and to all my Chinese and Vietnamese informants for their trust.

Funding

The fieldwork for the research presented in this article was made possible by the research funding provided by the Minerva Program of the Max Planck Institute for Social Research (Germany).

Notes

1. The Đong (VND) is the currency of Vietnam.
2. Van is Vietnamese but she resides in China (Dongxing), which allows her to open a Chinese bank account.

References

Abraham, Itty, and Willem van Schendel. 2005. "Introduction: The Making of Illicitness." In *Illicit Flows and Criminal Things: States, Borders, and the Other Side of Globalization*, edited by Willem van Schendel and Itty Abraham, 1–37. Bloomington and Indianapolis: Indiana University Press.

Barton, Clifton Gilbert. 1977. "Credit and Commercial Control: Strategies and Methods of Chinese Businessmen in South Vietnam." PhD diss., Cornell University.
Buskens, Vincent. 2002. *Social Networks and Trust*. New York: Kluwer Academic Publishers.
Chan, Yuk Wah. 2013. *Vietnamese-Chinese Relationships at the Borderlands. Trade, Tourism and Cultural Politics*. London and New York: Routledge.
Cheung, Siu Woo. 2000. "Regional Development and Cross-Border Cultural Linkage: The Case of a Vietnamese Community in Guangxi, China." In *Where China Meets Southeast Asia: Social and Cultural Change in the Border Regions*, edited by Grant Evans, Christopher Hutton and Kuah Khun Eng, 277–311. Singapore: Institute of Southeast Asian Studies.
Endres, Kirsten W. 2015. "Constructing the Neighbourly 'Other': Trade Relations and Mutual Perceptions across the Vietnam – China Border." *Journal of Social Issues in Southeast Asia* 30 (3): 710–741.
Hai, Chau Thi. 2000. "Trade Activities of the Hoa along the Sino-Vietnamese Border." In *Where China Meets Southeast Asia*, edited by Grant Evans, Christopher Hutton and Kuah Khun Eng, 236–253. Singapore: Institute of Southeast Asian Studies.
Horstmann, Alexander, and Reed L. Wadley. 2006. "Introduction: Centering the Margin in Southeast Asia." In *Centering the Margin: Agency and Narratives in Southeast Asian Borderlands*, edited by Alexander Horsmann and Reed L. Wadley, 1–24. New York and Oxford: Berghahn Books.
McMillan, John, and Christopher M. Woodruff. 1998. *Networks, Trust and Search in Vietnam's Emerging Private Sector*. Mimeo: University of California.
Misztal, Barbara A. 1996. *Trust in Modern Societies: The Search for the Bases of Social Order*. Cambridge: Polity Press.
Moore, Mick. 1999. "Truth, Trust and Market Transactions: What Do We Know?" *Journal of Development Studies* 36 (1): 74–88.
Parry, Jonathan P., and Maurice Bloch. 1989. "Introduction: Money and the Morality of Exchange." In *Money and the Morality of Exchange*, edited by Jonathan Parry and Maurice Bloch, 1–32. Cambridge: Cambridge University Press.
Peebles, Gustav. 2010. "The Anthropology of Credit and Debt." *Annual Review of Anthropology* 39: 225–240.
Stammler-Gossmann, Anna. 2012. "'Winter-Tyres-for-a-Flower-Bed': Shuttle Trade on the Finnish-Russian Border." In *Subverting Borders: Doing Research on Smuggling and Small-Scale Trade*, edited by Bettina Bruns and Judith Miggelbrink, 233–255. VS Verlag für Sozialwissenschaften / Springer Fachmedien Wiesbaden GmbH.
Tong, Chee Kiong. 2014. "Rethinking Chinese Business." In *Chinese Business. Rethinking Guanxi and Trust in Chinese Business Networks*, edited by Chee Kiong Tong, 1–20. Singapore: Springer.
Tong, Chee Kiong, and Pit Kee Yong. 2014. "*Guanxi* Bases, *Xinyong* and Chinese Business Networks." In *Chinese Business. Rethinking Guanxi and Trust in Chinese Business Networks*, edited by Chee Kiong Tong, 41–61. Singapore: Springer.
Wilson, Thomas M., and Hasting Donnan. 2012. "Border and Border Studies." In *A Companion to Border Studies*, edited by T. M. Wilson and H. Donnan, 1–25. West Sussex: Wiley-Blackwell.
Xie, Guangmao. 2000. "Women and Social Change along the Vietnam-Guangxi Border." In *Where China Meets Southeast Asia: Social and Cultural Change in the Border Regions*, edited by Grant Evans, Christopher Hutton and Kuah Khun Eng, 312–327. Singapore: Institute of Southeast Asian Studies.
Zhang, Juan. 2011. "Border Opened up: Everyday Business in a China-Vietnam Frontier." PhD diss., Macquarie University.

A tale of two borderlands: material lucidity and deep play in the transborder tourism space in Hong Kong and Macao[†]

Yuk Wah Chan

> This article examines post-colonial "development" of cross-border tourism at two border cities of China, Hong Kong and Macao, which returned their sovereignty to China in 1997 and 1999 respectively. Instead of considering such development merely a tourism feature, the author argues that the abundance of Chinese tourists to Hong Kong and Macao has resulted from the problematic growth of China. Transborder tourism space and relations between the two cities and China have signaled developmental flaws in China. While Hong Kong has become a remedy for China's "fake goods" market and has provided the opportunity for millions to seek "material lucidity," Macao has come to the rescue of China's outflow of *renminibi*, and acted as a space for the deep play of the risk-taking psyche of many mainland Chinese. The author concludes that these two border cities will continue to be "frontier thermometers" measuring the warm and cold "weathers" of China's transitional political economy.

Introduction

Hong Kong and Macao, two border cities at the southern margin of China, were reintegrated into China in 1997 and 1999 respectively. Despite the return of their sovereignty from the colonial powers of the British and the Portuguese to China, both cities have been allowed to retain their own social systems and economic structure to become two SARs under the "one country two systems" model. Borders are also maintained between China and the two cities. Despite this, since the late 1990s, Hong Kong and Macao have become increasingly integrated with China, especially in terms of the tremendous increases in tourist flows and cross-border interactions. This article[1] discusses two development positions peculiar to these two Chinese border cities. It examines how cross-border tourism (bringing in a few tens of millions of mainland Chinese to Hong Kong and Macao) developed into a full travel boom in the late 2000s. The policy that facilitated such development was the Individual Visit Scheme (IVS) implemented in the aftermath of the SARS outbreak in 2003. This policy allows citizens from selected provinces and cities in China to apply for individual permits to travel to Hong Kong. Prior to this, it would have been necessary for most Chinese nationals wishing to visit Hong

---

[†] A part of this article was presented at "Activated Borders: Reopenings, Ruptures, and Relationships," 4th Conference of the Asian Borderlands Research Network, held on 8–10 December 2014 at the City University of Hong Kong. The final version of the article has benefited much from the comments of two anonymous reviewers.

Kong or Macao to do so by way of package tours organized by travel agencies. With the convenience provided by this policy, millions of Chinese visitors now flock to Hong Kong and Macao every month.

Rather than perceiving the above as merely a tourist and leisure activity, this article argues that the abundance of arrivals of Chinese in these two border cities is an extension of problematic economic and social development in China. The extensive transborder interaction in cross-border tourism in Hong Kong and Macao has resulted from the following problems in China: (1) the prevalence of counterfeit goods and substandard products (including poisoned milk products); and (2) excessive wealth rendered by the transitional economy and the insecure development path in China that has led many to engage in risk-taking behavior acculturated in a high-risk and competitive social environment.

While millions of Chinese tourists have been eager shoppers in Hong Kong, many have been fervent gamblers in Macao, with both groups seemingly enjoying the privileges of shopping and gambling as their hobbies. News reports and market research surveys have focused on the enormous spending power in evidence, and highlight the flamboyant conspicuous consumption style of Chinese tourists. Nevertheless, few have offered succinct and deep analyses of the phenomena of shopping and gambling activities of the Chinese.

This article argues that the peculiarity of the boom in Chinese outbound tourism in Hong Kong and Macao is indeed an outgrowth of faulty development in China in the guise of tourism, with Hong Kong becoming a shopping haven (for safe and quality goods) and Macao a gambling sanctuary (a safer and more trustworthy environment for those seeking personal fortune and adventure). The lack of trust in the commodity world and the uncertainty and risks in the transitional political economy in China have both worked to push many to cross the border to find "material lucidity" and senses of assurance and security. Here material lucidity is defined as the senses of happiness and material assurance and gratification one obtains through attaining material goods perceived to be trustworthy and safe. Ulrich Beck (1992) has developed the concept of "risk society" to examine the social conditions produced by modernization. Besides encountering all sorts of environmental and health risks, risk societies also witness "lost security and broken trust in the human world that need to be addressed politically" (1992, 28). China, at the turn of the century, has ascended to the global political stage. Yet, the late development of China has garnered a prospering but risky social milieu, making many feel insecure. Being situated at the forefront margins (rather than the backyard) of China, Hong Kong and Macao have acted as "safety nets" through which China sieves the social and psychological tension of millions of Chinese. Letting these millions spend money in the two borderland cities also helps China to retain *renminbi* within the realm of its political regime.

Border relations and transborder development

Borderlands lie at the margin of the state and it is this marginality that allows border communities to develop beyond the possibilities provided by the state. The development of many borderlands in Asia has been the outcome of intensive interaction between border communities residing under two political regimes (Chan 2013; Evans et al. 2000; Horstmann and Wadley 2009; Pangsapa and Smith 2008; van Schendel and de Maaker 2014). Such communities make use of the differences across borders, which often include specialty goods, price differences, and different trade and tax policies, as resources for development, thus stimulating a thriving borderland economy. Their economic development also often incurs borderlanders' different ways of dealing with the authorities and challenging policies of the state. It is the marginality of such economies that allows them to circumvent the control and limits of the state. Some have pointed out how borderlands are riddled with informal and subversive economies, such as tax evasion and the smuggling of goods (Chan 2013; Hendrischke 2000; Wilson and Donnan 1999, 87–105).

The maintenance of the border between Hong Kong and China as well as that between Macao and China necessitates the maintenance of the status quo. While China has been reforming and integrating rapidly into the international capitalist system, it is largely still a transforming socialist economy ruled under an authoritarian one-party system. The "one country two systems" model has allowed Hong Kong and Macao to remain distinct from the rest of China. Besides maintaining the border between China and these two cities, the model also retains the cities' currencies (Hong Kong dollar and Macau pataca) and their financial systems. An important post-colonial feature in the two cities is the expansion of Chinese tourism, which has had an overall impact on the trans-border relationship. Chinese outbound tourism to the two SARs has directly boosted Hong Kong's retail commodity market and Macao's gaming economy. Cross-border shopping, tourism, and trading is commonplace in many borderlands. Existing literature has focused on how these economic activities have in general contributed to cross-border cooperation and borderland development (Bar-Kolelis and Dopierala 2014; Kovács 2013; Mihály 2011; Mumme 2015; Hampton 2010; Xheneti et al. 2013) and how increased interaction and integration has affected changes in consumer behavior (Bas and van de Velde 2008; Subramaniam et al. 2013). This article does not examine cross-border tourism in the light of tourism and economic development, but undertakes a deeper analysis to reveal how such cross-border tourism is an important indication of specific problems in the development model of China.

While Hong Kong has become a haven for Chinese consumers to seek "quality" goods, Macao has developed into a basin for excessive *renminbi*. Soon after its return to China, Macao became a fully developed gambling city, dubbed the oriental Las Vegas, with the consent and support of the Chinese government. Not only did the Chinese state explicitly support Macao's expansion of the gaming sector, it also helped to reduce triad influences and contain the spread of organized crime, which had long been embedded in the casino economy in Macao (Lo 2005).

Gambling is illegal in China and strictly forbidden by the state despite the great demand for Chinese to vent their lust for gambling. The prevalence of casinos mushrooming along the borderline around China proves the existence of such a vast market. It is a well-recognized fact that many individuals, finding nowhere to gamble and seek pleasures "safely" in China,[2] have found the gambling houses and brothels along the border regions between China and Southeast Asia to be highly accommodating (Chan 2008).

The Chinese authorities are not unaware of the outflow of *renminbi* to these borderland regions. Macao – lying close to and institutionally part of China – provides an alternative outlet for gambling among rich Chinese. Gaming taxes collected by the Macao government contribute to the economic prosperity and social welfare of Macao, which is a territory of China. Thus, Macao has played a role in retaining "gaming money" and controlling the outflow of Chinese currency.

Chinese outbound tourism and its development in Hong Kong and Macao

The development that has taken place in China over the past three to four decades has impressed the world, with its enormous manufacturing power and economic growth rates. China has also produced the largest number of outbound tourists in the world. Chinese cross-border tourism expanded tremendously in the decade of 2000 (CLSA 2005); the number of its outbound tourists grew from 10.5 million in 2000 to 107 million in 2014 (China Tourism Academy 2010, Travel China Guide 2015; Voellm 2011). Since 2012, China's outbound tourism has surpassed that of Germany and the US, to become the world's largest outbound tourism market. Chinese tourists have also become the top spenders in the world. In 2012, the spending power of Chinese tourists exceeded that of the Germans; in this year, they spent a total of US$102 million while visiting foreign destinations, with an average individual expenditure of US$1000 (China Tourism Update 2013; Cripps 2013; UNWTO 2013). Chinese tourists have also become very generous in consuming luxury products (CLSA 2011).

The rise of Chinese outbound tourism

There are a number of reasons for this tourism boom. In general, the increase of wealth among Chinese since the implementation of economic reforms in China has brought to many individuals and households disposable income for travel. Prior to outbound travel becoming a vogue, significant growth in domestic tourism was evident in China beginning in the 1990s. Indeed, the development of tourism in China has been a subject of state policies since the early 1990s.

In the 1980s, China was a country that tightly controlled its people's movements. Following the implementation of its opening up and reform policies, the market economy began to expand and de-collectivization set in. Since the 1990s, tourism has become a policy used to boost domestic market demands. This has been reflected in a number of policies, including one-week-long holidays (better known as Golden Week holidays) and the five-day working week (1995). The year 1996 was designated as the "Year of Leisure and Vacation." Together, these policies facilitated the growth of a leisure and travel culture in China, rationalizing leisure and travel activities for the benefit of both the people and the country's economy (Chan 2006; Nyiri 2006; Wen and Tisdell 2001). Also outbound travel has been promoted in recent years, necessitating the consent of tourist destinations regarding the easing of tourist visa requirements for the Chinese market.

The earliest Chinese outbound travel actually began in the early 1980s, when Chinese tourists were first allowed to visit Hong Kong (1983) and Macao (1984) in groups – by way of package tours arranged by travel agencies. The 1990s saw growth in cross-border tourism between China and a number of neighboring countries such as Mongolia, Vietnam, Laos, Burma and the former states of the USSR. Other early destinations for Chinese tourists were also in the Asian and Pacific regions and included Thailand (1988), Singapore and Malaysia (1990), the Philippines (1992), New Zealand (1998), Australia (1999) and Japan (2000) (Fan 2000; Zhang 1997; Zhang et al. 2003). Western countries initiated the issuing of tourist group visas for the Chinese in 2004 (CLSA 2005, 15). The US began to issue individual visas for Chinese tourists in 2006. In early 2012, President Obama announced the easing of steps on visa applications for travelers from China and urged government units to speed up visa processes in order to catch up with this lucrative market (Jansen 2012; The White House 2012).

While Chinese tourists are now found in almost every tourist destination around the world, the majority are in Asian destinations. Around 89.5 percent of outbound Chinese tourists chose Asian destinations for their visits in 2013, with Hong Kong and Macao accounting for around 70 percent of the total Chinese outbound market (Travel China Guide 2015). In 2014, Chinese tourists conducted a total of 47.2 million trips to Hong Kong (Hong Kong Tourism Commission 2015a) and 21 million to Macao (Nip 2015).

Chinese outbound tourism in Hong Kong and Macao

The "Individual Visit Scheme" (IVS) was implemented in late 2003.[3] The scheme facilitates the issue of entry permits to individual travelers from selected provinces and cities in China to travel to Hong Kong and Macao. As I have discussed elsewhere (Chan 2006, 2009), the IVS, besides being a new travel policy, also holds a symbolic meaning for Chinese travelers – to be free of the bondage of package tours (this is also why the scheme has been labeled with the colloquial term "free walk"). Prior to the implementation of the scheme, most Chinese tourists wishing to travel to Hong Kong and Macao had to join package tours organized by travel agencies. A number of cities in Guangdong province (such as Dongguan, Zhongshan, Jiangmen, and Foshan) were among the first to enjoy the privilege of "free walk." The scheme was later extended to other cities, covering a total of 49 cities by early 2015. Under the IVS, Chinese residents in selected cities can apply for a permit which will be valid for three months or one year (depending on the city); such a permit covers one or two visits, with each visit lasting a maximum of seven days (Hong Kong Tourism Commission 2015b).

Following the implementation of the IVS in 2003, the number of Chinese tourists to Hong Kong and Macao quickly doubled. In Hong Kong, the number of Chinese visitors increased from 6.82 million in 2002 to 12.24 million in 2004 (Hong Kong Tourism Board 2010). In 2014, the total number of incoming Chinese reached a record high, exceeding 47 million, and close to 60 percent of Chinese tourists in Hong Kong were same-day visitors (Hong Kong Tourism Commission 2015a). Macao had a similar experience; the number of Chinese visitors increased from 4.24 million in 2002 to 25 million in 2010 (Macau Business 2011). From there, the number continued to increase until 2013, when the Chinese authorities attempted to crack down on corruption and money-laundering. In 2014, total Chinese arrivals stood at 21.25 million (Macao Government Tourist Office 2015).

Among the tens of millions of Chinese tourists, many undertake such trips regularly – every few weeks or every few months. Permanent residents of Shenzhen, the Chinese city closest to Hong Kong have enjoyed the greatest level of privileges under the IVS. They were allowed multiple-entry to Hong Kong with their entry permits. However, such easy entry has created social problems; for example, the overwhelming number of travelers has placed significant stress on Hong Kong's transport facilities and encouraged parallel trading. In April 2015, the central government, at the request of Hong Kong, replaced the multiple entry policy with a "one trip per week" policy (Hong government 2015). Indeed, it is well-recognized that Chinese tourists love to travel to Hong Kong for shopping while many who visit Macao do so to visit the casinos. The following sections will examine how such frequent border-crossing activities have reflected the peculiar material desire and deep seated risk-taking behavior among much of the Chinese populace.

Transborder development and the shopping paradise in Hong Kong

Hong Kong first became known as a shopping paradise in the 1980s, when it began to cater to Western and Japanese tourists. Hong Kong, being a tax-free city and offering a wide variety of goods, has attracted many shopping-lovers for whom goods in Hong Kong are much less expensive than those found in their home countries. Since the early 2000s, Hong Kong has become a "paradise" for Chinese shopping "pilgrims." In addition to its cheaper goods, Hong Kong, compared to China, offers a greater sense of security in terms of the quality of goods.

Many news reports in the international media have highlighted the extraordinary spending power of Chinese tourists and how Chinese tourists are obsessed with the conspicuous consumption of world-branded luxuries. Yet, the majority of Chinese tourists actually do not engage in such conspicuous consumption. Instead, they engage in the random purchase of ordinary daily consumer products. Many are busy bustling in and out of supermarkets, medicine stores and skin-care chain stores in Hong Kong in order to purchase daily consumer items such as shampoo, toothpaste, detergent, diapers and baby food. Chinese tourists, especially those in Guangdong and other southern provinces who are eligible to apply for IVS permits, choose to cross the Hong Kong-China border on a regular basis to conduct this kind of shopping.

Modern Chinese "pilgrim" tourists

In tourism studies, Graburn (1978) has likened tourists to "modern pilgrims" who go on a trip periodically to leave their ordinary life behind. Rather than visiting sacred shrines or other such places as did pre-modern travelers, modern holidaymakers instead embark on "sacred" journeys to destinations where they can acquire new experiences and enjoy a period away from the mundane structure of their everyday lives. At the end of their trip, and following the modern spiritual "enlightenment" achieved during their liminal period of travel, they return home to incorporate themselves back into their normal routines. This is the "rite of passage" (van Gennep 1960) of modern tourists. Chinese tourists are also like modern pilgrims, although rather than taking a trip for the purpose of acquiring new experiences and cultural authenticity (MacCannell 1973), they cross the border to visit shopping centers for "material authenticity," and return home with bags and cases of "authentic" goods.

An important impetus that has pushed millions of Chinese to shop beyond China's border is linked to China's particular mode of production. Many Chinese, especially those who visit Hong Kong through the IVS on a regular basis, feel "addicted" or obliged to shop in Hong Kong because China itself is a haven for fake products. There is no doubt that China is the world's factory, but it is also notorious as a world center for the production of fake and copycat goods. CLSA, an investment consultant group, has estimated that China will become the world's largest luxury goods market by 2020. Over half of these goods will be bought outside China due to the "high tax rates" and "rampant counterfeit goods" found in China (CLSA 2011).

Counterfeit luxury goods only account for part of the story, however; a greater concern of the vast majority of Chinese relates to those fake consumer items and poisonous foods that cause health risks. Prior to 2009, the most purchased items among Chinese tourists we surveyed included skincare and cosmetics, luxuries (luxury brand products, gold and jewelry), medicine, clothing and shoes, daily consumer products (toothpaste, shampoo and bathing products), electronic products (phones and others) and baby milk powder.[4] However, since the outbreak of the milk scandal in late 2008, almost all Chinese tourists have felt obliged to take baby formula back home. At the completion of the 2008 Beijing Olympic Games, the milk scandal stirred up a whole whirlpool of food scares in China. Melamine-tainted milk products, especially in connection with baby formulas, contributed to 16 deaths and 300,000 sick infants (who were diagnosed with kidney and other health problems) (Li 2011; Shi 2008). Such food scares (mainly focused on milk and infant products) have directly led to Chinese people streaming out of the country to search for alternative products and, of all must-buy items, milk powder sits at the top of the list and is typically found among the suitcases and hand-carries of Chinese tourists in Hong Kong.

This seizing of baby formula by the Chinese led to severe milk shortages and angst among Hong Kong citizens by late 2010. Many rounds of social debates took place, urging the government to provide more milk and bring an end to the milk grab. Finally, in February 2013, the Hong Kong government, led by the present Chief Executive, Leung Chun Ying, announced a ban on the outflow of baby formula products from Hong Kong. Each tourist is now permitted to take back a maximum of two tins of baby milk powder from Hong Kong (Tsang and Nip 2013).

A free port since its establishment as a trading city in the mid-nineteenth century, Hong Kong, at the turn of the century, following the huge influx of Chinese tourists, thus implemented a policy that effectively bent Hong Kong's centuries-old philosophy of a free port, proud of its laissez-faire commercialist practices. Following the implementation of the policy, a number of mainlanders were caught by border customs officers exceeding the new 2-tin limit of baby milk products from Hong Kong, and were taken to court. Despite complaints voiced by Chinese tourists, the milk ban policy is still in place in Hong Kong. Moreover, Chinese citizens continue to cross the border for daily consumer items and milk powder, only now, because of the ban, young parents must cross the border even more frequently. Besides ordinary tourists who rush to Hong Kong to purchase milk powder for family use, there are a large number of people involved in "parallel trading," trying to smuggle baby formula of foreign brands across the border to sell to the vast market existing in China for foreign-made baby formula. By early 2015, some 9200 people had been arrested for breaking the baby formula law; two-thirds were mainland Chinese, the rest Hong Kongers. The new law does not seem to be much of a deterrent. During a court session convicting milk powder smugglers, a Hong Kong judge commented that such a state of affair was "a national disgrace" (Ong 2015).[5]

This peculiar lack of "material authenticity" is perhaps the most intriguing phenomenon in the Chinese model of development and production. It is true that China is the largest manufacturing power in the world, thus earning it the label of the "world's factory," but it is also producing many goods badly (Milder 2009). Whether low end or high end goods, many of the products bought by Chinese travelers to Hong Kong are actually produced in China and yet Chinese tourists are still willing to traverse the border in order to take them back home. This, again, is related to the problematic product quality checking/monitoring system in place in China.

As illustrated by Midler (2009), quality control in China quite often dissolves into non-existence for all sorts of economic and cultural reasons. While Hong Kong companies have a system that can better guarantee product quality prior to items being placed on retailers' shelves, unscrupulous Chinese manufacturers and distributors are continuously producing and selling copycat, substandard and fake products in the market in China (CSLA 2011). The commonly recognized fact that China is full of counterfeit and substandard products has pushed many mainlanders, especially those living in Southern China, to flock to neighboring cities such as Hong Kong and Macao to buy "authentic" medicine, milk powder, shampoo and toothpaste for themselves, their families, relatives, and friends. This discrepancy between the two sides has thus led to a peculiar kind of cross-border trade and business. Building on the above discussion, I now elaborate on the term "material lucidity," which I coin to examine the material aspirations and gratification of the mainland Chinese tourists who cross the border.

"Material lucidity" in transborder tourism space

Gaining insights from the narratives of the mainland Chinese tourists I interviewed in Hong Kong, I have coined the term "material lucidity" through which to analyze the earnest desire of Chinese visitors for authentic and safe goods, as well as the sense of happiness and assurance they enjoy through crossing the border. Such desire is particularly strongly cultivated among Chinese citizens due to the lack of sufficient trust of the quality control and production ethics in China. Everyday consumption has entailed "risk," and material gratification is delayed until one crosses the border. "Material lucidity" is thus a contrast to the "material murkiness" that exists in China, enshrined in the border space in between China and Hong Kong and evidenced by the footwork (crossing the border) of tens of millions of Chinese arriving in Hong Kong each year. Forged in the border space of Chinese outbound tourism is the belief in "authenticity" elsewhere and the distrust of inauthenticity at home. I have no intention of arguing whether material goods sold in Hong Kong are authentic or not, as "authenticity" is a constructed concept, both in material and cultural senses. There have been abundant debates on the concept of "authenticity" of cultural traditions and experiences (Appadurai 1986; Bruner 1994, 1991; Cohen 1988; MacCannell 1973). Authenticity is often negotiated in different social and cultural texts and shaped by subjective and existential positions (Pearce and Moscardo 1986; Olsen 2002). What is most important for the discussion here is the belief among mainlanders that material gratification lies across the border – a rite of passage to attain lucid/enlightened/assured material life. Many interviewees have illustrated this point with examples of manufactured medicine, shampoo, and diapers:

> We have used this brand of shampoo for many years already. Those bought in China are watery, and those bought here (Hong Kong) are thick.

> I can't be sure if the medicine we bought in China is fake or not, but the ointment from China can't cure our pain, whereas the same ointment bought in Hong Kong is very effective.

> My baby's skin is sensitive to China's diapers, and grows red dots. Diapers from Hong Kong make him comfortable…

> Yes, some people say this is psychological, but no one can prove this. We feel good using goods from Hong Kong.

In Mongkok, one of the busiest districts for shopping in Hong Kong, lined with a concentration of medicine shops, clothing boutiques, and cosmetic shops, one can easily spot Chinese tourists trying to open up and throw away the paper and plastic packages of the commodities they have just purchased in order to fit as much as possible into their suitcases and bags. Chinese tourists pulling fully loaded trolleys with bags of goods have become part of the peculiar city scene in Hong Kong. While interviewing tourists in Mongkok, I found that many actually had a list of items to obtain by the time they returned home later that same day. One 30-year-old woman said:

> I am busy, I have to buy a lot of things…Sure, 50 percent of the reason we are buying these things in Hong Kong is the abundance of fake goods in China.

Since 2013, the author has encountered an increasing number of young couples and young mothers who crossed the border to purchase milk formula and other baby products. The desire for safe baby food and products (such as effective diapers and cleaning agents) manifests a humble aspiration among post-1980s[6] young Chinese parents to cultivate their next generation (usually only one child for each young couple) in a healthy and happy manner. This humble desire pushes them to cross the border every few weeks to amass "material lucidity."

In the shopping mall in the Shatin district of Hong Kong, the author interviewed 20 young couples or mothers (all post-1980s generation) who travelled to Hong Kong every two to three weeks to buy milk powder and other goods. All interviewees stressed their priority goods to be baby items – milk powder, diapers and washing agents. If they had sufficient time, they would also shop for themselves, for items such as clothing, shampoo and cosmetics. One late evening, a young man in his late twenties, holding a can of milk powder in his arms which he had just purchased from Yatsue, the Japanese department store in Shatin, ran towards his young wife who was talking to me. I asked him, "Oh, you finally got it (the powder)?" He nodded happily, with a big smile. The glowing face of the young man stayed in my mind: all that was in his hands was not gold, but baby food.

I put the following question to my interviewees: "If every parent buys milk powder from abroad, who will consume China's own milk powder?" Many replied to this question with similar answers:

> We are the lucky ones; we can afford to get milk powder here. Those living in villages, or who live further away (towards the center of the country), or poor families, can't do what we are doing. Then their babies have to bear the risk: use China's milk powder.

One young mother said this to me:

> Ever since my baby was born, I have not for even one day let him drink milk powder from China. As long as we can afford this (crossing the border to Hong Kong to buy milk), we won't let our child take the risk. Adults like us may be able to endure those poisons, but not our baby. People in China have no morals. They put anything into the food. I was poisoned one time. I bought a can of milk for pregnant women from a big supermarket; not from a small stall, but a big market. After I opened the can and drank the milk, I found it had a strange taste and I felt sick. I asked the market to give me back the money, but they refused. They cheat people in all sorts of ways….

Another mainland woman emphasized the fact that she would not allow her baby to eat milk powder from China:

> In China, everything can be fake, and we are scared. Perhaps we, adults, can still bear the risks, but we can't let our babies take this risk.

A young mother carrying two cans of milk powder said:

> We are young, and our baby is just 14 months old. We don't want anything to happen to her. Since we live nearby, in Shenzhen, we can do this for our baby. I come over to Hong Kong every three weeks, but if my baby drinks a lot of milk, I may need to come even more frequently. If I can't come, I ask my colleagues or other friends, who come to Hong Kong to buy for me.

China's manufacturing power grew to an impressive level over the last two decades of the twentieth century. Chinese products fill almost every market in the world, and "made in China" has become a catchphrase in the world's economy. However, due to the rampancy of unethical production (Yan 2009), incidents of poisonous and fake food have regularly filled news reports in China, making international news headlines. A survey conducted by the Chinese Academy of Social Sciences shows that food safety sat within the top three worries of the Chinese public in 2011 (Yan 2012; Yang 2011). China's excessive manufacturing power has run awry and now encompasses all manner of unscrupulous manufacturing techniques. The peculiar mode of production and distribution of substandard products throughout China has wearied the minds of many Chinese, as illustrated above, and has generated much of the evident distrust surrounding the material world in China. The glowing smile of the young father holding a tin of milk powder indeed indicates an important "material lacuna" in China; and the material lucidity brewed in the border space between Hong Kong and China actually highlights China's ailing manufacturing industry and problematic material world, shaping and shaped by a politics of difference produced at the border.

Transborder development and the gaming economy in Macao

This section seeks to elaborate upon the restructuring and development of the gaming economy in Macao within the context of its relationship to Chinese gambler visitors. It argues that this particular postcolonial development of the borderland economy in Macao has not only contributed towards the prosperous boom of Macao's economy, but has also benefited China in terms of providing an outlet for the excessive wealth produced in its transitional economy. Macao houses China's only legal casino industry, which is largely fed by serious high-roller gamblers from China. The thriving gaming regime is thus an extension of China's imbalanced "political economy." While there is no perfect solution by which China can control all channels of outflow of *renminbi*, having the easily accessible Macao on its doorstep does, to a certain extent, aid the Chinese government in its desire to retain a significant proportion of the money generated in China's booming economy, especially that proportion pocketed by corrupt officials. An expert[7] on Macao's gaming economy has commented in an interview with me,

> Prior to the return of Macao to China, Macao's reserves were only 1 billion (MOP); a decade after its return, its reserves amounted to 100 billion (MOP). This demonstrates well the money-power of gambling. With this money, Macao has become extremely prosperous, but it is beneficial to China too; at the very least, rich cadres and businesspeople spend their money in the region rather than in Las Vegas or the borderland casinos of Vietnam, Burma and Cambodia.

In China, casino gambling is forbidden by law. However, the Chinese authorities were very supportive of the glamorous postcolonial development of Macao from a casino backwater into a grand "Las Vegas" in the Orient. On the day following the establishment of the Macao SAR government, Ho Hau Wah, the new Chief Executive of Macao (in 1999), announced his plan to bring an end to the monopoly within the gaming sector. Prior to this, Macao's casinos were operated by STDM (Sociedade de Turismo e Diversões de Macau), a gambling concessionaire established in 1962 that had monopolized Macao's gaming industry for 40 years (Gaming Inspection and Coordination Bureau 2015).

In August 2001, the Macao government passed the "Legal Framework for the Operations of Casino Games of Fortune" (No. 16/2001) law, setting out the legal requirements and eligibility criteria of major casino shareholders and management, as well as the conditions for submitting gaming taxes. Moreover, with the objective of attracting new investment and injecting fresh dynamics into the gaming industry, the Macao SAR government decided to grant three new gaming concessions upon the expiry of the STDM license at the end of 2001. This new policy boosted Macao's gaming economy tremendously and steered Macao onto an irreversible path – an explosion of casino construction and new gaming structures (Rose 2010). By 2014, Macao had six gaming concessionaires, including gaming giants from the US, Hong Kong and Macao, and a total of 35 casinos (Gaming Inspection and Coordination Bureau 2015).

It is no secret that the prosperous gaming economy in Macao has been largely fed by Chinese visitors. While there are millions and millions of Mainland Chinese visiting Macao and its casinos every year, not all of them are frequent visitors. Some follow packaged tours and table a few casual bets at the casinos. Yet, there are hundreds of thousands of frequent gamblers who enter Macao easily from Guangdong province with the IVS permit.

The majority of the gamblers I interviewed were from the southern provinces, including Guangdong, Fujian, Hunan, and Sichuan. A Sichuan man told the author, "I won around $40,000. Look here, I bought this watch with the money." The Sichuan man immediately drew some attention from the people around us, and he said that he visited Macao every few months. Two young Chinese ladies who worked in a foreign company frequented Macao's casinos with the intention to win some lucky money to buy things. They told me that they aimed at buying new mobile phones on that trip. Being asked what if they lost, one of the ladies replied without hesitation: "let it be." A group of co-workers of different ages from Hunan went to the casinos in Macao every two months. I asked them why they came to Macao so often, and one of them told me, "Chinese men are like this, they like to have fun together…gambling is fun and excitement."

On top of petty gamblers, there are also high rollers – those who make high-stakes bets. The gaming revenue of Macao has mainly been the result of high-stakes gambling – i.e. games in VIP rooms.[8] The following sections will examine high-stakes gambling and the junket system that has linked the border city's gaming scene to the millions of extremely rich Chinese who dwell in different areas of China. It was through this system that Macao's casino concessionaire was able to reach out to the "hidden tigers and dragons" in China, who subsequently brought their fortunes to the gambling tables of Macao. This section will also examine the reasons why so many Chinese engage in cross-border gambling. Rather than explaining this away by stating that "Chinese like gambling," I argue that gambling, and high-stakes gambling in particular, is indeed "deep play" (Geertz 1973), reflecting the deep-seated "risk taking" behaviors prevalent in China's unstable political economic structure throughout the opening and reform eras.

VIP rooms and high-stakes gambling

While casinos in the West rely heavily on slot machines and table games for revenues, Macao's casinos operate quite differently. The industry places significant stress on the development of VIP gambling: the games of high-stakes gamblers. Revenue from VIP rooms accounts for 65–72 percent of the total gaming revenue each year in the decade after Macao opened up the market (Deutsche Bank 2012; Gaming Inspection and Coordination Bureau 2014; Wang 2014). Moreover, as analyzed by Wang (2014), unlike the operation of the VIP rooms in other countries (where casino operations provide a direct premium to promoters), the VIP rooms within Macao's casinos are contracted to a third party which is believed to be able to bring in high rollers, or high-stakes gamblers, to the casino.

This third party can be either a corporation or a person, who will sign a contract with a casino concessionaire. The contract designates the conditions and obligations of both sides, such as the minimum quantity of chips to be sold by the VIP-room contractor, the rate of commission for the contractor, and other remuneration that a contractor can extract from the sales, as well as certain monetary punishments imposed on the contractor if the set sales goals are not achieved (Wang and Zabielskis 2010, cited in Wang 2014). These contractual conditions, including the monetary awards and punishments, impel contractors to work hard in their search for wealthy gamblers for the casinos (Wang 2014).

In Macao, this contractor offers junkets. Junket companies are registered by law as "gaming promoters." The regulation of junket companies through their institutionalization represents a new pathway for the Macao government, since the return of its sovereignty. Junket companies hire a large number of collaborators or customer representatives, or outsource their work to sub-agents, to reach out to potentially significant gamblers throughout the vast territory of Mainland China, as well as to neighboring regions such as Hong Kong, Taiwan and Japan. The work of VIP-room contractors and their cooperators is often so effective that each party is able to bring millions of dollars' worth of gambling money into the casinos. Therefore, a VIP room is not just an individual compartment of a casino in which high-rollers may gamble, but is rather a powerful vehicle by which casinos and gaming promoters can make money (Wang 2014; Wang and Eadington 2007).

The junket system and China's networked society

The junket system works by outsourcing the services of catering to big stakes gambling to third parties – junket companies – who will in turn reach out to potential big rollers. It is a highly efficient and culture-sensitive system, enabling gambling corporations to reach out to all sorts of potential VIP guests throughout China's interior. All kinds of business in China has been conducted through myriad personal connections – *guanxi* (Gold 1985; Gold et al. 2002; Gomez and Hsiao 2001; Pearson 1997; Wank 1999, 2000, 2003). *Guanxi* is also essential for the gaming business. It would be difficult for Macao-, Hong Kong-, and US-based companies to reach out to the vast gambling market in China without middlemen and agents. Indeed, in the early days when US casino operators first opened their businesses in Macao, they did not accept the VIP junket system. It was only after seeing their VIP rooms empty for a year that they began to succumb to the junket system and its Asian method of operation (Lee 2011, 33–34).

Junket operators are often agents from China who are hired by or are connected to a vast pool of subagents, who then stream out to link up with potential high-stakes gamblers or "bosses" who are looking for venues in which to gamble and seek out "pleasures." Many of these sub-agents, or marketing representatives, are "floaters" looking for any chance at money-making, including by illicit means. Through inter-personal link-ups, these agents can be posted to deep interior provinces of China – such as Heilongjiang, Shangtong and Shaanxi – to locate gamblers.

While there are many billionaires in China, they need to be linked to Macao through middlemen that they know and trust. Cross-border gambling is still largely "taboo," especially for cadres and officials. Only through interpersonal linkages can junket operators gain the trust of these potential customers. Moreover, junket operators are professionals who are knowledgeable about all the games in the casinos, and thus can act as advisers to novice gamblers.

Besides marketing gambling to Macao's casinos, many junket companies also operate full-service travel agencies that primarily serve the gaming market (Lee 2011). They can offer all manner of conveniences for the travel and border-crossings of their clients but their most important role is to provide their customers with unlimited chips. In order to facilitate the non-stop play of big rollers, junket companies prepare pools of gambling chips for the VIPs to gamble with. China has imposed strict limits on the amount of cash that Chinese nationals can remove from the country. Thus, it is important for junket operators to be able to provide an enormous quantity of chips for the pleasure of VIPs. To the casino corporations, this is a sensible and culture-sensitive way of attracting high rollers and has proven to be an efficient and clean way of handling the high-stakes gaming business. By outsourcing the VIP rooms to junket companies, the casinos have also channeled out the risks involved in the sector. The VIP customers are directly handled by the junkets, who have myriad ways of collecting debts owed by customers. The casino corporations therefore need not get their hands "dirty" in the course of debt collection.

A junket's subagent from Shangtong told me that he had lived on commissions from bringing in big gamblers since 2006. People like him have all levels of social networks (from officials and cadres to all kinds of entrepreneurs closely related to the state-led neo-liberalist economy) and are sufficiently mobile to travel to remote areas for the purpose of linking up with the rich people of those areas. He said that many corrupt officials in China had a great deal of money to spend but gambling often led to great monetary losses for gamblers. He had seen people losing many millions of *reminbi*, and was also aware of some who had committed suicide. Although he himself would definitely never gamble, he would not persuade others not to do so.

> If they don't gamble, we don't have rice to eat.[9] I won't stop them. Sometimes that serves them right. They took all the pretty girls in China as wives and lovers, leaving us none…

The expansion of China's economy from the 1990s through to the 2010s produced millions of extraordinarily rich people – both businesspeople and cadres – who in turn have contributed to the explosion of the gaming economy in Macao and elsewhere through their gambling. Before Macao even became the Oriental Las Vegas, gambling houses had already mushroomed in the borderlands between China and Southeast Asia. Most visitors to these gambling dens are from China. Some countries, such as Vietnam and Cambodia, prohibited their own nationals from entering the casinos; the casinos were built solely to serve foreigners, especially the Chinese. The Chinese state was not unaware of how Chinese nationals had been fervently engaging in cross-border gambling. Thus, Chinese crackdowns on outbound travel aimed at gambling were sporadically carried out. In the Vietnam-China borderlands, it was said that a high-powered camera was set up at the border in an effort to trace high-ranking officials who gambled across the border. Thus, many gamblers chose to use alternative paths to cross the border "illegally." Local people believed that crackdown activities would only last for a short while and there would not be long-term committed efforts to curb corruption in China; and indeed, after some actions, the situation returned to "normal," people returned to crossing the border as usual and casinos once again saw the crowds (Chan 2013).

It is well-recognized that a proportion of high-stakes gamblers have been betting away money from the public pocket or money accumulated from corruption. Money laundering in Macao has thus occasionally made news headlines (Badkar 2013; Carvalho 2015; Lopez 2015; Reuters 2015; The Standard 2013). Anti-graft campaigns enforced by the Chinese authorities have often had a direct effect on the revenues of the gaming economy. Since Xi Jinping, the current Chinese President, came to power, his consistent fight against corruption and extravagance among communist cadres has shaken the junket economy and Macao's gaming industry, and an increasing number of junket operators have announced the closure of VIP rooms. News reports also describe how the once bustling scenes of VIP rooms have become stagnant (Forbes 2015; Macau Business Daily 2015; Wong 2015a, 2015b).

This is quite an ironic situation. On the one hand, China has supported Macao to become the only territory in China to run a legalized gaming industry, allowing it to fully develop into an Eastern gaming hub. China is well aware of the fact that it is only with the participation of the big rollers from China that the gaming sector in Macao can prosper. On the other hand, the Chinese authorities are politically obliged to combat corruption and corruption within the Chinese bureaucratic system cannot be allowed to run awry; thus, it has to sporadically crack down on corrupt and extravagant practices.

Macao has indeed provided an outlet in which corrupt officers can spend their excessive money. As argued by an expert[10] on the gaming economy in Macao, if Macao had not provided this large basin through which to sieve the huge reservoir of money from the black economy of China, these pools of money would have flowed to other gambling dens around China or elsewhere. Junket operators in Macao have already threatened to take their clients to other casinos in Northeast and Southeast Asia, as countries in the region have all tried to ease visa requirements for Chinese nationals and have eyed this lucrative market (Stradbrooke 2015; Wong 2015b).

The development and evolution of transborder relations within such a gambling space seem to be inevitable developments. While China is striving to correct the wrongs in its fast-developing economy, it certainly cannot stamp out corruption overnight. Before China can boast a relatively clean government, it would have to discontinue its production of large troupes of big rollers attempting to find excitement through high-stakes gambling, and melting their corrupt money into gambling chips through baccarat games. Having Macao at its margins to sieve corrupt elements and retain the *renminbi* flowing out of the boundaries of China is perhaps one possibility for mending the flaws within the political economy of China.

Gambling fever and the risk-taking culture in China

Many have attributed gambling fever to a "primordial" feature of the Chinese – i.e. the Chinese are by nature gamblers. While it is difficult to prove or disprove this attribute, this section attempts to undertake a structural analysis of Chinese gambling, examining gambling behavior in the context of unstable socio-economic development in post-reform China.

Basu (1991), in her analysis of the gambling behaviors of overseas Chinese entrepreneurs in Calcutta, found that gambling, besides its function as a social gathering event, also reflects the nature of entrepreneurship. She likens gambling to entrepreneurship, both of which depend very much on fate and involve high-level risk-taking. Ozorio and Fong (2004) surveyed the risk-taking behavior of Chinese gamblers in Macao's casinos and found that the desire for instant rewards and quick profits may explain gamblers' irrational risk-taking behavior. They also liken this irrational risk-taking behavior to that of investors in China's stock markets.

China's four decades of "openness and reform" have led the country to progress from an extremely poor country to the second largest economy in the world, and have produced an enormous amount of wealth. At the same time, they have produced myriad "unstable" avenues to the gaining of such wealth. In the Chinese transitioning economy, there were all sorts of trial-run policies. A policy promoted by the state one day could become a source of illicit economic dealings the next. One needs to take bold steps and make timely decisions in order to grasp the economic opportunities offered by "openness and reform." It is also important to make the correct choices in exploiting the political economic situation and to build the right *guanxi* network to exploit such opportunities and avoid risks. A *guanxi* network could be seen as an essential source of power and an avenue to wealth one day, and a source of trouble the next. Making these choices is high-risk; one may easily fall prey to the inconsistent and unstable developing economy and power structure in China.

In my study of cross-border business and gambling in the China-Vietnam borderland (Chan 2013), I argued that post-reform China is a particularly hot stove for brewing risk-taking behavior. High-stakes gambling is indeed a reflection of the collective psyche in the rapidly transforming Chinese society. To place high-stakes bets on the gaming table is not unlike taking a gamble amidst sporadic policy changes in the investment and business environment, and the complexly institutionalized *guanxi* networks in China (Chan 2013, 104):

> [T]he post-socialist economy in China is still much embedded in the mix of *shuren jingji* and *guanxi*, which comprises different forms of patron-client ties, semi-open markets and state-dictated policies. Because of the need to open and reform, someone had to put forward bold polices to help break away from state-tied economic operations. However, one also has to bear big political and economic risks in doing so.... In the decades of the 2000s, bureaucratic directions in China had not diminished, but had only diversified into a range of coercive state-society ties. In China, where the structured economy has been intertwined with many unknowns and sporadic changes in the patron-client relationships that one is obliged to enter into, people are under constant pressure to make risky decisions. A sense of insecurity and uncertainty about policy changes and ups and downs in the clientele system means that nothing can be 'for sure'. *Shuren*, after all, may turn into *diren* (enemies).... As both businesspeople and gamblers have stressed to me, in China, one needs to take risks (*yao buo*) and act daringly (*yao danzi da*) if one would like to be successful.

I met Ling, a woman from Heilongjiang in her late 40s, in the Venetian casino in Macao, when she was picking up lottery cards abandoned by other gamblers. She was once a worker in a mining company but was laid off in the late 1980s. She then started up her own wedding-gown and photography shop, and made a fortune. That day, Ling had lost quite some money. I invited her to join me for a simple meal at the café in the casino, and she told me her story:

> In China, it was not difficult to make an easy fortune as long as you were bold and started up a business at the right time. Then, you could not go further, because there was more and more competition. Then you had to think up other ways to make profits. One always has to take risks. Gambling is one way. Before visiting Macao, I had gambled in the underground gambling den in Heilongjiang but they are bad people; they cheat. Some friends told me that casinos in Macao do not cheat; one depends on one's fate. That's why I am here. I have been here for almost a year. When my visa expires, I return to Shenzhen and get a new entry stamp, or fly to Thailand and then come back. There is no difficulty. Most of the time I lose, but sometimes I win… It is useless to feel regret in this situation… I need to win back the money I have lost here; at least one-third of the money. Then, I will return home and never gamble again. My son has not married yet, and I need to have some money to give him a good wedding…
>
> How much do you earn in Hong Kong? How high is Hong Kong's salary? Right; it is hard for you Hong Kong people to understand us, to understand a situation where people go hungry. Now, in my situation I cannot return. To return home and make a thousand a month? I won't reconcile with that…I saw many people gamble away lots and lots of money. Sometimes I want to tell them not to gamble, but if I can't even convince myself not to gamble, how can I convince them?

Since Macao's return to China, transborder interaction has developed at full swing, with a tremendous increase in both the number of casinos and the number of Chinese visitors. The development of the gaming economy in the border city of Macao has taken place together with the ups and downs of the political economy in China, and the different fates of many small and large entrepreneurs and workers from China. Thus, gambling and the lust for risk-taking among Chinese is "deep play" (Geertz 1973), reflecting a high-risk society in the evolving political economy of China. In the age of "openness and reform," China is full of opportunities and yet it is also replete with risks and dangers. Geertz (1973, 412–453) has studied the cockfight in Bali. Instead of seeing it merely as a leisurely gambling activity among village men, he argues that "it is not only apparently cocks that are fighting there…it is men" (Geertz 1973, 417). Through placing bets on the cocks, which command deep psychological identification with Balinese men, clans and families come to resolve tensions and conflicts. In the age of "openness and reform," China is full of opportunities and yet, it is also replete with risks and dangers. High stakes bets placed on gambling tables reflect the deep structural risks generated in the transitional economy in China. Gambling is only one of the ways that men and women from China are allowed play out the uncertainty and tension in their social and economic life.

Conclusion

Since 1997 and 1999, Hong Kong and Macao have respectively traversed an irreversible path of reintegration with China despite the fact that both were promised a certain degree of autonomy under the "One Country Two Systems" model. The few tens of millions of Chinese nationals entering Hong Kong and Macao each year represent a social phenomenon beyond tourism. The analysis in this article has indicated that such a development reflects the problematic transitional political economy in China. While Hong Kong has become a haven for tens of millions of Chinese to fetch quality goods, and to channel their desire for "material lucidity" through cross-border shopping, Macao has become a haven for channeling the gambling lust of Chinese. Rather than seeing the participation of Chinese people in gambling as a tourist activity, the author provides an alternative perspective, highlighting casino gambling as "deep play" of Chinese society. It reflects the collective risk-taking psyche commonly found among the Chinese in post-reform China, which has produced uncertainties alongside stability and wealth. In a nutshell, crossing borders has become a survival strategy of many Chinese to mend the flaws in the development of China.

Notes

1. This article is a result of the author's ongoing research on the development of Chinese outbound tourism. Most of the interviews of tourists in Hong Kong were conducted in the summer of 2013 and spring of 2014, while the interviews of tourists in Macao were conducted in 2011 and 2012 during two field trips to Macao.
2. Informants told the author that in spite of strict state control on gambling, underground gambling dens permeate China. Those who frequent such gambling houses in China run the risk of being arrested.
3. Earlier that year, the SARS outbreaks killed in excess of 100 people in Hong Kong; in addition to the human cost, the economy was also badly affected.
4. This data was gathered by the author and her research team in the summer of 2008 in the Mongkok district of Hong Kong. A total of 82 mainland Chinese tourists were interviewed.
5. In addition to tourists crossing the border to fetch milk powder, there are thousands of people engaging in parallel trading, one of the most criticized informal economic practices at the Hong Kong-China border. Many of these petty traders supply baby formula and other products for retailers at *ganghuo dian* (shops selling commodities from Hong Kong) in China. The *ganghuo dian* phenomenon is yet another intriguing social scene in China which requires further research.
6. This means people born in the 1980s.
7. The interview was conducted by the author on 25 May 2012 at the University of Macao (also see Index Mundi 2015; Landers 2008).
8. Each bet in the VIP rooms is often over Hong Kong $1million, which is around US $125,000. See Willett (2013).
9. This line is translated directly from the Chinese "*meifanchi*.".
10. See note 8.

References

Appadurai, Arjun. 1986. "On Culinary Authenticity." *Anthropology Today* 2 (4): 25.
Badkar, Mamta. 2013. "How China's Filthy Rich Use Macau to Launder Their Money." *Business Insider*, 11 November. Assessed August 23, 2015. http://www.businessinsider.com/how-people-use-macau-to-launder-money-2013-11.
Bar-Kolelis, Delia, and Lukasz Dopierala. 2014. "Ukrainian Cross-border Shoppers Influence at the Polish and Romanian Borders: A Comparative Study from Suceava and Lublin." *Romanian Review on Political Geography* 16 (2): 78–87.
Bas, Spierings, and Martin van de Velde. 2008. "Shopping, Borders and Unfamiliarity: Consumer Mobility in Europe." *Journal of Economic and Social Geography* 99 (4): 497–505.

Basu, Oxfeld E. 1991. "Profit, Loss, and Fate: The Entrepreneurial Ethic and the Practice of Gambling in an Overseas Chinese Community." *Modern China* 17: 227–259.

Beck, Ulrich. 1992. *Risk Society: Towards a New Modernity*. London: Sage Publication.

Bruner, Edward. 1991. "Transformation of Self in Tourism." *Annals of Tourism Research* 18 (2): 238–250.

Bruner, Edward. 1994. "Abraham Lincoln as Authentic Reproduction." *American Anthropologist* 96 (2): 397–415.

Carvalho, Raquel. 2015. "US Lawyer Handling Ng Lap Seng's Bribery Case Could be Ace in the Hole." *South China Morning Post*, 25 October, A1.

Chan, Yuk Wah. 2006. "Coming of Age of the Chinese Tourists: The Emergence of Non-Western Tourism and Host-guest Interactions in Vietnam's Border Tourism." *Tourist Studies* 6 (3): 187–213.

Chan, Yuk Wah. 2008. "Fortune or Misfortune? Border Tourism and Borderland Gambling in Vietnam." In *Asian Tourism: Growth and Change*, edited by Janet Cochrane, 145–155. Oxford: Elsevier.

Chan, Yuk Wah. 2009. "Disorganized Tourism Space: Chinese Tourists in an Age of Asian Tourism." In *Asia on Tour: Exploring the Rise of Asian Tourism*, edited by Tim Winter, Peggy Teo, and T.C. Chang, 67–78. London: Routledge.

Chan, Yuk Wah. 2013. *Vietnamese-Chinese Relationships at the Borderlands: Trade, Tourism and Cultural Politics*. London: Routledge.

China Tourism Academy. 2010. *The Annual Report of China Outbound Tourism Development*. Beijing: China Tourism Academy.

China Tourism Update. 2013. "Chinese Tourists' Overseas Expenditure Reach USD102 Billion in 2012." 24 June. Accessed July 12, 2015. http://www.tldchina.com/EN/WebSite/yudu.aspx?id=2248&FID=445.

CLSA. 2011. *Dipped in Gold: Luxury Lifestyles in China*. Hong Kong: CLSA.

CLSA. 2005. *Chinese Tourists: Coming, Ready or Not!* Hong Kong: CLSA.

Cohen, Erik. 1988. "Authenticity and Commoditization in Tourism." *Annals of Tourism Research* 15: 371–386.

Cripps, Karla. 2013. "Chinese Travelers, the World's Biggest Spenders." *CNN*, 12 April. Accessed July 12, 2015. http://edition.cnn.com/2013/04/05/travel/china-tourists-spend.

Deutsche Bank. 2012. *Macau: Frontier Country Report*. 27 June.

Evans, Grant, Christopher Hutton, and Kuah Khun Eng, eds. 2000. *Where China Meets Southeast Asia: Social and Cultural Change in the Border Regions*. Singapore: Institute of Southeast Asian Studies.

Fan, S. Chengze. 2000. "Economic Development and the Changing Patterns of Consumption in Urban China." In *Consumption in Asia: Lifestyles and Identities*, edited by Chua Beng-Huat, 82–97. New York: Routledge.

Forbes. 2015. "Casino Notes: Macau Gaming Revenues Plunge 37% in May." *Forbes*, 2 June. Accessed September 4 2015. http://www.forbes.com/sites/greatspeculations/2015/06/02/casino-notes-macau-gaming-revenues-plunge-37-in-may/2/.

Gaming Inspection and Coordination Bureau (Macao SAR Government). 2015. "Macao Gaming History." Accessed August 23, 2015. http://www.dicj.gov.mo/web/en/history/.

Gaming Inspection and Coordination Bureau (Macao SAR Government). 2014. "Gaming Statistics." Accessed August 23, 2015. http://www.dicj.gov.mo/web/en/information/DadosEstat/2014/content.html#.

Geertz, Clifford. 1973. *The Interpretation of Cultures: Selected Essays*. New York: Basic Books.

Gold, Thomas. 1985. "After Comradeship: Personal Relations in China since the Cultural Revolution." *The China Quarterly* 104: 657–675.

Gold, Thomas, Doug Guthrie, and David Wank, eds. 2002. *Social Connections in China: Institutions, Culture, and the Changing Nature of Guanxi*. New York: Cambridge University Press.

Gomez, Edmund Terence, and Hsin-Huang Hsiao. 2001. "Chinese Business Research in Southeast Asia." In *Chinese Business in Southeast Asia: Contesting Cultural Explanations, Researching Entrepreneurship*, edited by E.T. Gomez and Hsiao Hsin-Huang, 1–37. Surrey: Curzon.

Graburn, Nelson. 1978. "Tourism: the Sacred Journey." In *Hosts and Guest: The Anthropology of Tourism*, edited by Valene Smith, 17–31. Oxford: Blackwell.

Hampton, Mark P. 2010. "Enclaves and Ethnic Ties: The Local Impacts of Singaporean Cross-border Tourism in Malaysia and Indonesia." *Singapore Journal of Tropical Geography* 31: 239–253.

Hendrischke, H. 2000. "Smuggling and Border Trade on the South China Coast." *China Perspectives* 32: 23–35.

Hong Kong Government. 2015. "Press Release: Hong KongSAR Government Welcomes New Measure to Optimise 'Multiple-entry' Individual Visit Endorsements." 13 April. Accessed August 23, 2015. http://www.info.gov.hk/gia/general/201504/13/P201504130887.htm

Hong Kong Tourism Board. 2010. "Tourism Statistics". Accessed August 23, 2015. http://partnernet.hktb.com/pnweb/jsp/comm/index.jsp?charset=en.

Hong Kong Tourism Commission. 2015a. "Tourism performance in 2014". Assessed August 23, 2015. http://www.tourism.gov.hk/english/statistics/statistics_perform.html.

Hong Kong Tourism Commission. 2015b. "Individual Visit Scheme." Assessed September 24,2015. http://www.tourism.gov.hk/english/visitors/visitors_ind.html.

Horstmann, Alexander, and Reed L. Wadley. 2009. *Centering the Margin: Agency and Narrative in Southeast Asian Borderlands*. New York: Berghahn Books.

Index Mundi. 2015. "Macau Economy Profile." 23 August 2015. http://www.indexmundi.com/macau/economy_profile.html.

Jansen, Bart. 2012. "Obama Eases Visa Rules to Boost U.S. Tourism." *USA TODAY*, 19 January. http://travel.usatoday.com/news/story/2012-01-18/Obama-expected-to-shorten-tourist-visa-process/52652668/1.

Kovács, András. 2013. "On Borders, Border Regions and Cross-border Retail-trading." *Scientific Papers of the University of Pardubice* 20 (28): 29–42.

Landers, Jim. 2008. "What's the Potential Impact of Casino Tax Increases on Wagering Handle: Estimates of the Price Elasticity of Demand for Casino Gaming." *Economics Bulletin* 8 (6): 1–15.

Lo, Shiu Hing. 2005. "Casino Politics, Organized Crime and the Post-Colonial State in Macau." *Journal of Contemporary China* 14 (43): 207–224.

Lee, Ben. 2011, June. "The Easternization of the West: A Perspective on Western Views on Asian Gaming Operations." *Global Gaming Business*: 30–33.

Li, Joseph. 2011. "Demand Grows for Action over Milk Powder Shortage." *China Daily*, 29 January.

Lopez, Linette. 2015. "Chinese Gangster 'Broken Tooth' is Back in Macau, and No One Understands How It Happened." *Business Insider*, 26 June. Accessed October 20, 2015. http://www.businessinsider.com/broken-tooth-reportedly-opens-macau-vip-room-2015-6.

Macau Business Daily. 2015. "Two More Junkets Shutting Down VIP Rooms." 2 August. Accessed September 4, 2015. http://macaubusinessdaily.com/Gaming/Two-more-junkets-shutting%C2%A0down-VIP-rooms.

Macau Business. 2011. "Macau Received 25 Million Tourists in 2010." 20 January. Accessed June 12, 2015. http://www.macaubusiness.com/news/macau-received-25-million-tourists-in-2010/7075/.

Macao Government Tourist Office. 2015. "Tourism Statistics." Accessed June 12, 2015. http://industry.macautourism.gov.mo/en/Statistics_and_Studies/list_statistics.php?id=39,29&page_id=10.

MacCannell, Dean. 1973. "Staged Authenticity: Arrangement of Social Space in Tourist Settings." *American Journal of Sociology* 79 (3): 589–603.

Mihály, Tömöri. 2011. "The Role of the 'DebOra' Cross-Border Eurometropolis in the Hungarian-Romanian CBC Relations: A Case Study of Shopping Tourism in Debrecen and Oradea." *Eurolimes* 11: 170–178.

Milder, Paul. 2009. *Poorly Made in China: An Insider's Account of the China Production Game*. Hoboken, NJ: John Wiley & Sons.

Mumme, Stephen. 2015. "Sustaining the Borderlands in the Age of NAFTA: Development, Politics, and Participation on the U.S.-Mexico Border." *Review of Policy Research* 32 (6): 745–746.

Nip, Amy. 2015. "Macau Tourist Arrivals up 7.5 Per Cent amid Fall in Gambling Revenue." *South China Morning Post*, 21 January. Accessed September 21, 2015. http://www.scmp.com/news/hong-kong/article/1688347/macau-tourist-arrivals-75pc-amid-fall-gambling-revenue.

Nyiri, Pal. 2006. *Scenic Spots: Chinese Tourism, the State, and Cultural Authority*. Seattle, WA: University of Washington Press.

Olsen, Kjell. 2002. "Authenticity as a Concept in Tourism Research: The Social Organization of the Experience of Authenticity." *Tourist Studies* 2 (2): 159–182.

Ong, Larry. 2015. "In 2014, 9,200 People Tried to Sneak 90 Tons of Baby Formula from Hong Kong." *Epoch Times*, 10 February. Accessed October 12, 2015. http://www.theepochtimes.com/n3/1245729-in-2014-9200-people-tried-to-sneak-90-tons-of-baby-formula-from-hong-kong/.

Ozorio, Bernadete, and Davis Ka-Chio Fong. 2004. "Chinese Casino Gambling Behaviors: Risk Taking in Casinos vs Investments." *Gaming Research and Review Journal* 8 (2): 27–38.

Pangsapa, Piya, and Mark J. Smith. 2008. "Political Economy of Southeast Asian Borderlands: Migration, Environment, and Developing Country Firms." *Journal of Contemporary Asia* 38 (4): 485–514.

Pearce, Philip, and Gianne Moscardo. 1986. "The Concept of Authenticity in Tourist Experiences." *Australia and New Zealand Journal of Sociology* 22 (1): 121–132.

Pearson, Margaret. 1997. *China's New Business Elite: The Political Consequences of Economic Reform*. Berkeley: University of California Press.

Reuters. 2015. "Macau Arrests 17 in Money Laundering Crackdown as China Downturn Fears Grow." 26 August. Accessed September 21, 2015. http://www.reuters.com/article/2015/08/26/us-macau-crackdown-idUSKCN0QV07Q20150826#a2PrpicwVmydKl3t.97.

Rose, Melson. 2010. "Gambling and the Law: The Explosive But Sporadic Growth of Gambling in Asia." Accessed September 21, 2015. http://www.gamblingandthelaw.com/index.php?option=com_content&view=article&id=252:the-explosive-but-sporadic-growth-of-gambling-in-asia&catid=3:recently-published-articles&Itemid=8.

Shi, Jiacuang. 2008. "China's Baby-milk Scandal: Formula for Disaster – the Politics of an Unconscionable Delay." *The Economist*, 18 September.

Stradbrooke, Steven. 2015. "Macau Junket Brace for Impacts from Room Closures, Visa Restrictions." 10 June. Accessed September 21, 2015. http://calvinayre.com/2015/06/10/casino/macau-casino-junket-investors-brace-for-impact/.

Subramaniam, Thirunaukarasu, Evelyn S. Devadason, and Sivachandralingam Sundararaja. 2013. "Cross-Border Shopping: Examining Motivations from the Perspective of Bruneian Visitors in Limbang, Malaysia." *Jurnal Ekonomi Malaysia* 47 (1): 21–30.

The Standard. 2013. "Las Vegas Gambling Official Says Macau Casino VIP Rooms in the Grip of Criminals." *The Standard*, 28 June. Accessed September 21, 2015. http://www.thestandard.com.hk/breaking_news_detail.asp?id=38152.

The White House. 2012. "Executive Order - Establishing Visa and Foreign Visitor Processing Goals and the Task Force on Travel and Competitiveness." Office of the Press Secretary, 19 January. Accessed February 27, 2015. http://www.whitehouse.gov/the-press-office/2012/01/19/executive-order-establishing-visa-and-foreign-visitor-processing-goals-a.

Travel China Guide. 2015. "China Outbound Tourism in 2014." Accessed 23 August 2015. http://www.travelchinaguide.com/tourism/2014statistics/outbound.htm.

Tsang, Emily and Amy Nip. 2013. "Two-can Limit on Milk to Stop Cross-border Traders." *South China Morning Post*, 2 February. Accessed September 4, 2015. http://www.scmp.com/news/hong-kong/article/1141498/two-can-limit-milk-powder-stop-cross-border-traders?page=all.

UNWTO. 2013. "Press Release: China's New National Tourism Strategy Set to Increase Outbound Tourism." 25 March. Accessed August 23, 2015. http://media.unwto.org/en/press-release/2013-03-25/china-s-new-national-tourism-strategy-set-increase-outbound-tourism.

Van Gennep, Arnold. 1960. *Rites of Passage*. Chicago, IL: University of Chicago Press.

Van Schendel, Willem and Erik de Maaker. 2014. "Asian Borderlands: Introducing their Permeability, Strategic Uses and Meanings." *Journal of Borderlands Studies* 29(1): 3–9.

Voellm, Daniel. 2011. *The 21st Century Game-Changer Up Close – China Outbound Tourism*. Hong Kong: HVS.

Wang, Changbin. 2014. "Licensing VIP-Room Contractors or Gaming Promoters in Macao: The Status Quo and Improvement." *UNLV Gaming Research & Review Journal* 18 (2): 105–111.

Wang, Wuyi, and William R. Eadington. 2007. "VIP-room Contractual System of Macau's Traditional Casino Industry." UNR Economics Working Paper Series, Working Paper No. 07-001.

Wank, David. 2003. "Business-State Clientelism in China: Decline or Evolution?" In *Social Connections in China: Institutions, Culture, and the Changing Nature of Guanxi*, edited by Thomas Gold, et al., 97–115. New York: Cambridge University Press.

Wank, David. 2000. "Cigarettes and Domination in Chinese Business Networks: Institutional Change during the Market Transition." In *The Consumer Revolution in Urban China*, edited by Deborah Davis, 268–286. Berkeley: University of California Press.

Wank, David. 1999. *Commodifying Communism: Business, Trust, and Politics in a Chinese City*. Cambridge: Cambridge University Press.

Wen, J., and C. Tisdell. 2001. *Tourism and China's Development: Policies, Regional Economic Growth and Ecotourism*. Singapore: World Scientific.

Willett, Megan. 2013. Inside the Macau Casino VIP Room Where the Minimum Bet is $1.6 Million, *Business Insider*, 29 May. Accessed August, 23 2015. http://www.businessinsider.com/inside-the-macau-casino-vip-room-2013-5.

Wilson, Thomas M., and Hastings Donnan. 1999. *Borders: Frontiers of Identity, Nation and State*. Oxford: Berg.

Wong, Stephanie. 2015a. Empty VIP Tables in Macau Means Trouble for $44 Billion Industry, *Bloomberg News*, 3 February. Accessed August 23, 2015. http://www.bloomberg.com/news/articles/2015-02-03/empty-macau-vip-tables-show-slide-in-44-billion-industry.

Wong, Stephanie. 2015b. "Macau Junket Operator David Group to Close Some of Its VIP Rooms." *Bloomberg News*, 17 January. Accessed August 23, 2015. http://www.bloomberg.com/news/articles/2015-01-17/macau-junket-operator-david-group-to-close-some-of-its-vip-rooms.

Xheneti, Mirela, David Smallbone, and Friederike Welter. 2013. "EU Enlargement Effects on Cross-border Informal Entrepreneurial Activities." *European Urban & Regional Studies* 20 (3): 314–328.

Yan, Yunxiang. 2009. "The Good Samaritan's New Trouble: A Study of the Changing Moral Landscape in Contemporary China." *Social Anthropology* 17 (1): 9–24.

Yan, Yunxiang. 2012. "Food Safety and Social Risk in Contemporary China." *Journal of Asian Studies* 71 (3): 705–729.

Yang, Jian. 2011. "Costs, Food Safety Top List of Worries." *Shanghai Daily*, 20 December.

Zhang, Guangrui. 1997. *Zhongguo bianjing luyou fazhan de zhanlue xuanze* [The strategic choices of the development of border tourism in China]. Beijing: Jingji Guanli Chubanshe.

Zhang, Qiu, Carson L. Jenkins, and Qu Hailin. 2003. "Mainland Chinese Outbound Travel to Hong Kong and its Implications." In *Tourism in China*, edited by Alan Lew, Yu Lawrence, Zhang Guangrui and John Ap, 277–286. New York: The Haworth Hospitality Press.

Index

Note: Page number in *italic* type refer to figures
Page numbers followed by 'n' refer to notes

Abraham, Itty, and van Schendel, Willem 76
absolute space 34
actor-oriented approach 2–3
agents of vice 66
Akha people 58, 60–62, 64; Administration 71; Self-administered Division 71; Self-determination 71
amphetamine type stimulants (ATS) 70–71
anthropology of borderlands 1–2
Arduous March (1995–1998) 22, 27, 29, 35n1
Asian Development Bank (ADB) 40
asymmetries 2–3, 5
authenticity 99

Bangkok dream 45
Bao Youxiang 68
Barton, Clifton Gilbert 86
Basu, Oxfeld E. 106
Battlefield Quemoy 16
Beck, Ulrich 93
black/brown regions (Myanmar) 58, 63–64
Bloch, Maurice, and Parry, Jonathan P. 85
blurring boundaries 46–47
Boot, W. 65
border areas 4, 6, 10–12, 16–17, 38–40, 42, 48, 67, 76; framing 13–14; normal 13, 16; as venues of interactions 11–12, 16–17
border relations 93–94
border venue 12–13, 17
border-crossing 1, 3–6, 22–23, 26–29, 32–34, 40, 58, 62, 64, 66, 69, 77, 96, 104; gate 67–68; un-institutionalized 4
borderland prototypes 5
borderlands studies 61–63
borders-in-transition 3
boundaries 1, 4, 39, 58, 105; blurring 46–47
brothels 72, 94
brown/black regions (Myanmar) 58, 63–64
Burma: Communist Party of Burma (CPB) 58–59, 63, 67; Socialist Programme Party (BSPP) 40, 63, 72n2

business 15; ethics 76, 80, 82, 86, 88
Buskens, Vincent 86

capabilities, asymmetries of 10, 17–19, 20n2
capital, trust 6, 86–89
ceasefire agreements, Myanmar 41, 49–50, 58–61, 63–65, 67
central government, Myanmar 46, 49, 58, 60, 63–66
Chan, Yuk Wah 2, 7, 39, 62, 92–112; and Womack, Brantly 1–9
Chao Ngi Lai 68
Chen Shui-bian 20
Chiang Kai-shek 15, 17
China, People's Republic of (PRC) 5, 16–17, 19–20, 71; Fujian 14–16, 19; Guangdong 15–16, 81, 96–97, 102; *guanxi* (personal relations) 87, 103, 106; Guomindang (KMT) 14, 19–20; map *14*; milk scandal (2008) 98; Ming Dynasty 15; networked society 103–105; political economy 5, 7, 92–93, 101, 105, 107; Qing Dynasty 15–16, 19; risk-taking 7, 92–93, 96, 102, 105–108; Yunnan 58, 60, 62, 68–69, 72
Chinese, Han 30–33
Chinese Academy of Social Sciences (CASS) 101
Chinese Communist Party (CCP) 67
Chinese outbound tourism 93–94, 99, 108n1; in Hong Kong and Macao 96; rise of 95–96
Chu, Eric 20
CLSA 97
Cold War (1947–1991) 1, 11, 16–17, 33–34
Cold War Island (Szonyi) 16
Communist Party of Burma (CPB) 58–59, 63, 67
Companion to Border Studies, A (Wilson and Donnan) 76
control, border 4, 25, 27, 41
Convention of Beijing (1860) 19
Convention Relating to the Status of Refugees (1951) 42, 46

113

INDEX

cooperation, trustful 75–76
cost-benefit perspective 23
coup d'état, Thailand 39, 50–52
Cunningham, Hilary, and Heyman, Josiah 39

Dannecker, Petra, and Schaffar, Wolfram 6, 38–57
delayed payments 81–82, 87–88
Democratic Progressive Party (DPP) 17, 20
difference 17–19; gradient of 11–13, 16–17
Do Casinos Cause Economic Growth? (Walker and Jackson) 66
Đổi Mới policy (1986) 87
doing borders 39, 49, 52
Dongxing 75–76, 83
Dongxing-Móng Cái Free Trade Zone 75
Donnan, Hastings, and Wilson, Thomas M. 3–4, 76
Dork Niw Kham (Golden Niw Flower) 66
Dulles, John Foster 15
Durbar meetings 66–67

economic crisis, North Korea 22, 25–26, 28–29, 34
economy: borderlands 64–70, 94, 101; fragile balance of 76–79
Endres, Kirsten W. 89
ethics, business 76, 80, 82, 86, 88
everyday space 24, 26, 34

fake goods 7, 92
female jobs 29
feminization, of North Korean mobility 28–29
Ferguson, James, and Gupta, Akhil 39
fight back ideology 5
Fish, Shrimp, and Crab (game) 67
Fong, Davis Ka-Chio, and Ozorio, Bernadete 106
Foreign Employment Act (Thailand, 1978) 42
foreign policy 13
formal migrants 40
Four Cuts anti-insurgency strategy 50
framing 13–14
free walk 96
Fujian 14–16, 19

gambling 62, 64–67, 93–94, 101, 108, 108n2; fever 105–107; high-stakes 102–107
Gambling on Law Lessness (Boot) 65
Geertz, Clifford 107
gender 28–30, 33
Geneva Convention (1949) 42, 46
GI Joe business 15
Golden Rule 17, 19
Golden Triangle 66
Golden Week (holidays) 95
government 2
Graburn, Nelson 97

Grillot, Caroline 6, 75–91
Guangdong 15–16, 81, 96–97, 102
guanxi (personal relations) 87, 103, 106
Guomindang (KMT) 14, 19–20
Gupta, Akhil, and Ferguson, James 39

Han Chinese 30–33
Hegelian triad 10–13, 16, 20n1
Henders, S. J. 71
Hess, Sabine, and Tsianos, Vassilis 44
Heyman, Josiah, and Cunningham, Hilary 39
high-stakes gambling 102–107
hill-tribe ID cards 51–52
Ho Hau Wah 102
Hong Kong 7, 11–12, 15, 42, 58, 96
Horstmann, Alexander 39
Horstmann, H. 24
human trafficking 31, 42, 45, 51

ID cards, hill-tribe 51–52
identities, differentiation of 12–13
illegal migrants 27, 33, 40, 45–46, 48, 51–52
Individual Visit Scheme (IVS) 92, 96–97, 102
industrialization process 38, 40
informal border exits 4
informal migrants 40, 46
interests, differentiation of 12–13
Irrawaddy 65

Jackson, J. D., and Walker, D. M. 66
junket system 102–105
junta 43, 51–52

Kachin Independence Army 40, 71
Kachin State (Myanmar) 41, 58, 63, 68
Karen National Union (KNU) 40, 41, 49–50
Karen people 40–41, 44, 46, 49–50, 53n3, 58
Karen State (Myanmar) 41, 58
Keng Tong 60–61, 63
Kennedy, John F. 15
Khin Nyunt 50
Kim, Sung Kyung 6, 22–37
KoKang 59–60, 63–64, 68, 71, 72–73n10
Korean War (1950–1953) 28

labor migrants 38, 42–43, 49
Lahu people 58, 60–62, 64
Lee, Sang Kook 45, 53n4
Legal Framework for the Operations of Casino Games of Fortune (2001) 102
legal migrants 27, 40, 52
legalization 4
Leiper, N. 64
Leung Chun Ying 98
life experiences, of North Korean women 30–33
Lippmann, Walter 15
Luohei people 60–61
Lwe people 58

INDEX

Macau 7, 58, 62, 65–66, 71, 96, 102
McGowan, Richard A. 66
McMillan, John, and Woodruff, Christopher M. 87
Mae Sot (Myanmar) 40–42, 44–46, 48–49, 52, 53n4
Mandala 61
material: authenticity 97–98; lacuna 101; murkiness 99
Meehan, Patrick 49
Memorandum of Understanding (MOU) 43, 48
Midler, Paul 98
migrants: formal 40; illegal 27, 33; legal 27
military *coup d'état* (Thailand) 39, 50–52
milk powder shortage 98–101, 108n5
milk scandal, China (2008) 98
Ming Dynasty 15
mini-three links policy 16, 20
Ministry of Progress of Border Areas and National Races and Development Affairs (Myanmar) 65–66
Mintz, Sidney W. 39
Misztal, Barbara A. 86
mobility 4, 39, 42–43, 48; North Korean 6, 22–23, 25–29, 28–29, 34; two regimes of 44–46
Moei River 44
Móng Cái (Vietnam) 6, 75–76, 80, 83, 86, 88–90; Central Market 77, 78, 79, 81–83, 87; little Wall Street 6, 82–86
Mong La: Burma's City of Lights (Williams) 65
Moore, Mick 79
Muse 63
Myanmar Kings 60
Myawaddy (Myanmar) 44, 51

National Archives (Myanmar) 63
National Council for Peace and Order (NCOP) 51
National Democratic Alliance Army (NDAA) 58
National League for Democracy (NLD) 47
nationality verification 43, 47–49, 51–52
networked society, China 103–105
Nixon, Richard 15
non-governmental organizations (NGOs) 41, 44, 47
North Hamgyong Province (North Korea) 23–24, 26–28, 34
North Korea: economic crisis 22, 25–26, 28–29, 34; North Hamgyong Province 23–24, 26–28, 34; Pyongyang 27–28; women 30–33
Nyiri, Pal 62, 65, 68

Obama, Barack 95
one country two systems model 92, 94, 107
one trip per week policy 96
Ong, Aihwa 39, 49

open borders 3
openness and reform, China 106–107
opium 61–64, 67–68; fall of production 70–71
outbound tourism, China 93–96, 99, 108n1
Ozorio, Bernadete, and Fong, Davis Ka-Chio 106

Pang Sang 61, 63
parallel trading 96, 98, 108n5
Parry, Jonathan P., and Bloch, Maurice 85
patriarchy 29–30, 32, 34
payments, delayed 81–82, 87–88
Peebles, Gustav 81
People's Liberation Army (PLA) 14
People's Republic of China (PRC) *see* China
People's Volunteer Army (Pyithu Sit) 63
pilgrim tourists 97–99
Pingtan Island 16
place/space framework 2, 29
political economy, China 5, 7, 92–93, 101, 105, 107
power, landscape of 39–45
Prayut Chan-o-cha 48, 51
prostitutes 33, 72
Protocol Relating to the Status of Refugees (1967) 42, 46
Pyongyang (North Korea) 27–28

Qing Dynasty 15–16, 19
Quemoy 1, 5–6

reactivated border zones 4–5
Red Shirts (Thailand) 50
reflexivity 17–18
reforms, Myanmar 47–50
relative space 34
Republic of China (ROC) *see* Taiwan
Restoration Council of Shan State (RCSS) 70
restrictive borders 3
risk society 93
risk-taking, China 7, 92–93, 96, 102, 105–108
Rohingya Muslims 43, 52
Rozenberg, Danielle 62

sacred journeys 97
Sai Lin 58, 65, 68, 70
SARS outbreak (2003) 92, 108n3
Say Htin 68
Schaffar, Wolfram 49; and Dannecker, Petra 6, 38–57
Schendel, Willem van 62; and Abraham, Itty 76
Schengen Area 13
Scott, James 12, 43, 48
securitization 42
security issues 39, 41, 51
Shan people 41, 60–62, 64, 70
Shan Sawbwas (hereditary chieftains) 60

INDEX

Shan State (Myanmar) 58, 60, 63–64, 66–68, 71; Army 40; Eastern 58, 60, 63–64, 68; Northern 60, 63, 68, 71; Southern 60
shopping paradise 97–101
Skinner, G. William 12
social costs, casinos 71–72
Sociedade de Turismo e Diversões de Macau (STDM) 102
Soe Lin Aung 38, 48
sovereignty 1, 3–4, 24–25, 49, 61, 66, 68, 76, 92, 103
space/place framework 2, 29
Special Administrative Regions (SARs) 7, 92, 94
Special Economic Zones (SEZs) 49–52
state economy 71
State and Law Council (Burma) 41
State Law and Order Restoration Council (SLORC, Burma) 63, 72n1
synesthetic trick 62
Szonyi, Michael 15–16

Taing Ne 60
Taiwan (Republic of China) 5–6, 11, 15–17, 19–20, 42, 103; map *14*
Taiwan Strait 1, 16–17
Tak Province (Thailand) 48–49, 51
Tan, Danielle 49
Thai-Myanmar Friendship Bridge 44–46
Thaksin Shinawatra 48, 50
Than, Tharaphi 6, 58–74
Thein Sein 47–48, 51
thereness (border area) 13
Thompson, Sally 41–42
Tong, Chee Kiong 86–87
tourism, Chinese outbound 93–94, 95–96, 99, 108n1
tourists, pilgrim 97–99
trading, parallel 96, 98, 108n5
trafficking, human 31, 42, 45, 51
transborder development: and border relations 93–94; and gaming economy 101–107; and shopping paradise 97–101
translocal border space 4
Treaty of Shimonoseki (1895) 19
trustful cooperation 75–76
Tsai Ing-wen 20
Tsianos, Vassilis, and Hess, Sabine 44
Tsou, Tang 15
Tumen River 24–27
Twelve Animals Top (game) 67

un-institutionalized border-crossing 4
undocumented migrants 42–43, 45, 47
United Nations High Commissioner for Refugees (UNHCR) 42, 46
United Nations Office on Drugs and Crime (UNODC) 70
United States Navy (USN) 19
United Wa State Army (UWSA) 71
United Wa State Party (UWSP) 67
Universal Coverage Scheme 51

venue of interactions 11–12, 16–17
Vietnam 6, 11, 19, 62, 104–106, *see also* Móng Cái
VIP rooms, casinos 69, 102–105, 108n8

Wa people 59–61, 63, 67–68
Walker, Andrew 62
Walker, D. M., and Jackson, J. D. 66
Wang, Changbin 103
War Zone Administration 15
wasteland 40
Western Taiwan Strait Economic Zone 16
Williams, J. 65
Wilson, Thomas M., and Donnan, Hastings 3–4, 76
Womack, Brantly 5–6, 10–21; and Chan, Yuk Wah 1–9
Woodruff, Christopher M., and McMillan, John 87
Woods, Kevin 49
World War, Second (1939–1945) 59

xenophobia 50–52
Xi Jinping 105
Xiamen 14, 16–17
xinyong (trust) 75, 86–88

Yanbian Korean Autonomous Prefecture 24, 26–27
Year of Leisure and Vacation (1996) 95
Yellow Shirts (Thailand) 50
Yingluck Shinawatra 50
Yu, Keping 2
Yunnan 58, 60, 62, 68–69, 72

Zahkung Ting Yang 68
Zhang, Juan 76
Zhu Yihai 15
Zomia 61–62